This book is a great read for peopec-
dotes are entertaining and heart\   hat
learning life's lessons at a young a

    —Renee Foster
    Owner, Picture Perfect Productions

Memories of my own childhood during the 1950s came flooding back
to me as I read this book. Anyone who grew up in that time period will
identify with the author's experiences and get a good laugh at the same
time!

    —Heather S. Nelson
    Homemaker

Delightfully entertaining from cover to cover.

    —Renee Whitely
    Secretary/Treasurer, Guthriesville Tire & Service

I relived my youth–a great treasury of stories.

    —Carl Linsenbach
    Owner, Eastern Consolidation & Distribution
    Services, Inc.

My children and I thoroughly enjoyed the book. We enjoyed Ken's
refreshing and heartwarming stories of his early childhood.

    —Jennifer Dull
    Homemaker

A refreshing journey of a little boy's adventures during his age of
innocence.

    —Judy Anderson
    Sales Assistant, Salvation Army

Sweet Freedoms

Sweet Freedoms

50
Life Lessons
from Life in the '50s

Shocking True Stories You Can Tell Your Grandkids

Ken Gaudi

HIGHERLIFE

DEVELOPMENT SERVICES, INC

Oviedo, Florida

Sweet Freedoms: 50 Life Lessons from Life in the '50s
by Kenneth E. Gaudi

Published by HigherLife Development Services, Inc.
400 Fontana Circle
Building 1—Suite 105
Oviedo, FL 32765
(407) 563-4806
www.ahigherlife.com

Disclaimer: These stories happened more than fifty-five years ago but are my recollection of how these events occurred. While each of the stories shared are based on truthful circumstances, a few of the stories may have been enhanced with additions or may have happened at a later date. Some names have been changed for failure to receive permission to use their name, and other names have been changed to protect parties involved.

ISBN 13: 978-1-935245-19-3
ISBN 10: 1-935245-19-8

Cover Design: Judith McKittrick Wright

First Edition

10 11 12 13 — 9 8 7 6 5 4 3 2 1

Printed in the United States of America

Dedication

Dedicated to all my grandchildren.

Table of Contents

Acknowledgements

I wish to thank you for letting me share some of my childhood stories that have been brought to life by writing this book. I hope you enjoy reading the book as much as I enjoyed writing the book. It brought back the simple pleasures and fond memories of my childhood. This book would never have been written without the encouragement of my grandchildren Colton and Chase Dull for providing the idea to write my childhood stories. Without the assistance from Renee Foster, Sue Ciarimboli, Emily Stambaugh, Kay McKinney, Paul Timashenka, and Cindy Dlugolecki, this book could not have been written. Special thanks go to my wife Peggy for her encouragement and support to complete my book.

Introduction

Approximately three years ago while having lunch at McDonald's, my two grandkids, Colton and Chase (then ten and six) asked me what my all-time favorite fast food restaurant was when I was growing up. I replied that it was called "Mom's Restaurant." The grandkids said they never heard of a restaurant by that name. I explained to them that we didn't have fast food restaurants while I was growing up. My grandkids said, "No sir, PapPap," and laughed. I explained to them that Mom's Restaurant was the kitchen in our home, where my mother cooked every meal every day for our family. I then explained to them that I never went out to eat in a restaurant until I went to college. It was hard for them to believe, and they laughed!

I then told them how I walked more than two miles to school and back every day—rain, snow, cold, or shine—from third grade until I finished eighth grade. We had no bus transportation. My father drove to work, my mother didn't drive, and we only had one car. Since they ride the bus to school, it was hard for them to comprehend. Again they didn't believe me and laughed.

So I then explained to them that we didn't have TV or DVDs or PlayStation to watch or play. We almost always played outside.

No TV or PlayStation for PapPap. None! Again they were amazed. "No sir, PapPap!"

I also told them the story of how I climbed a tree and with the help of friends jumped down on a cow and rode it for a couple of feet before it bucked me off. I did it because of a double dare. I had to explain to them that during those days we never backed down from a double dare. Again they laughed and didn't believe me.

They were so taken with my stories that they begged me to tell them one more story before we left the restaurant. So I told them how I grew up leaving the house on summer mornings around 8:00 a.m. and not returning until 5:00 p.m. for dinner. I didn't have to call my mother, and my mother never worried about me. Once again they were in disbelief and laughed. What a wonderful lunch the kids and I had that day.

Two weeks later Colton and Chase were at my home and asked me to tell them another story from when I was their age. They wanted a funny one. They also wanted a scary story, and I obliged them. Both stories left them laughing and in disbelief. They had no idea being a kid could be so much different for me than it is for them. I had no idea that they would be that interested or entertained by my recollections.

As we were finishing playing cards that day, they asked me for another story. I said, smiling, "I'm all out of stories." But as they looked at me, I decided to get serious with them. I told them to remember this important rule of life—the most important things in life are family and friends. And if you do remember this rule, I assured them, happiness would find you.

After they went home that evening, I thought about writing some short stories about my childhood before I would forget or lose interest. I'm grateful for the life lessons I've learned, and I will be glad if my grandchildren and others find them as useful and practical—and as enjoyable and meaningful—as I have.

I was told once that life is like a roll of toilet paper: the closer it gets to the end, the faster it goes. A few days after my conversations with the boys, still contemplating my idea, I decided to document my experiences as a youth so my grandchildren and their children could better understand and perhaps appreciate how I lived and grew up during that period of time (1949-54), a special era of American life. As a result, I've developed this book of my childhood experiences and lessons learned in hopes that readers will find it enjoyable and good to know that the simple pleasures of life are filled with great lessons, which are important parts of the "Sweet Freedoms" we can all enjoy.

Chapter 1

High Park, Pennsylvania: My Boyhood Home

I was born on July 13, 1944—during World War II. These key years of my childhood, between 1949 through 1954, provided me with the core values that have made me who I am today. They were years filled with life lessons involving success, failure, responsibility, relationships, cooperation, death, change, and acceptance. These lessons, formed through my experiences with my family, friends, teachers, and others in my community, helped develop my morals, values, and qualities of my personality.

I grew up in High Park, a blue-collar neighborhood next to the city of Jeannette in western Pennsylvania located approximately thirty miles east of Pittsburgh. The city of Jeannette during the early 1950s was a thriving industrial town of approximately 18,500 people. Glass making was a major reason for its existence. In 1950 the Jeannette Glass Company, where my father worked, was the largest window glass factory in the world, employing more than one thousand people (History of Jeannette—Bicentennial–American Legion Post 344– published 1976).

The small community of High Park had a population of approximately 150 people. This hamlet, during that era, was what I consider an "All-American Community." High Park, as the name suggests, was nestled above the city of Jeannette on a plateau with a slight sloping landscape east to west. Located to the west and southwest lay a large cluster of trees surrounded by open fields. Some of the larger green pastures just west of our community was used to fatten cows, and a slaughterhouse and butcher shop were also located on the farm property. Other adjoining pastures were used for dairy farming and corn crops. Beyond those fields were large, rolling, tree-filled hills dotted with additional fields.

The kids in our High Park community claimed two fields, which we used exclusively for play. One was a baseball/softball field; the other was what we called our football/army field. These fields provided High Park's young people with a safe place to meet, play, and hone our athletic skills. Surprisingly no one ever broke a leg or arm; maybe we were just lucky.

While we played, our fathers worked at a plant or store, and our mothers worked at home. During the fifties the city of Jeannette had several major glass plants, a rubber and plastic plant, and even a brewery. In other words, the majority of people went to work each day and made something real, something you could touch. It was not a "virtual" world.

The thriving downtown area included, among other things, banks, clothing stores, furniture stores, hardware stores, appliances stores, movie theaters, schools, churches of all denominations, gas stations, a brewery, a newspaper office, a post office, a car dealership, a rail line, and a streetcar service that ran though the main street of town.

There were no indoor shopping malls. On Fridays and Saturdays the streets were filled with people walking and carrying shopping bags. The main street, Clay Avenue, was the hub of human activity. On Sundays all the downtown stores were closed, and the town was at ease. Sunday was family day, and most families went to church.

The majority of our fathers in High Park worked in one of the aforementioned plants. As I recall, nobody earned a great deal of money, and we, the High Park kids, didn't fully realize that most of the families living in our community were by most standards lower middle-class. But we had food, clothing, and shelter. What else did we need? We were happy. For us kids, money was not an issue during this period of our lives. We had none. Our world was extremely small. When people mentioned Pittsburgh, we thought of it as a city on the other side of the world. It was rare for any of us to travel very far at all outside our neighborhood.

Lesson #1: Humble beginnings can be good beginnings (and they are nothing to be ashamed of).

Families in High Park were a cohesive unit; few mothers, if any, worked or drove a car. Most were stay-at-home moms. I can't remember any parents getting a divorce in our neighborhood. It just didn't happen. Although families didn't socialize much, we all knew each other.

The families of High Park all had modest homes, and everyone drove used cars. No one that I remember owned a new car. Few homes had a garage, but we were fortunate to have a detached two-car garage. The priorities of that era were to put food on the table, then pay the mortgage and utility bills. Because of their experiences going through the Depression, most parents hid extra money in the house for emergencies. Others put their spare money in a savings account at the bank.

The High Park families were of mixed descent—Italians, Irish, Polish, and Germans. My dad was Italian, and my mother was Irish and German. In our neighborhood, if we misbehaved in the community parents would quickly receive a phone call from an adult. God forbid that your father received a call. Adults and teachers were always right. The corporal punishment was swift and severe. My father was tough but fair. If a neighbor would say to us (no matter how caught up we were in any kind of rowdy fun), "I am going to call your father if you don't stop doing that right now," we immediately quit what we were doing. Any phone call to a parent from another neighborhood adult produced genuine fear. We knew the likelihood of punishment, so the threat brought results 99.9 percent of the time.

Our parents, in particular, prohibited profanity or swearing. My father warned us about swearing. I never slipped, because I knew the consequences. I could see it in his eyes when he warned me not to do something. I listened. At times we would swear among our friends, but it wasn't a good practice because of the fear of slipping and having to face Dad's corporal punishment.

Looking back, it's a little bit strange to think that these rules against swearing were enforced by the same people who did most of the profanity we heard. At this early age, any swear words we knew we learned from our fathers. They were great teachers. Few, if any, mothers ever used profanity. When my father started working on a project, whether it was a car repair or fixing something around the house, he would inject these "unholy" words into his work if things didn't go right. But he never used God's name in vain. I'm proud to say that I didn't learn the serious cuss words from my father. I did surprisingly enough learn those words while attending grade school.

Generally, High Park families led a very scheduled life. Fathers left for work early in the morning with their lunch-pails in hand and returned home between 4:00 p.m. and 5:00 p.m., depending on their scheduled shift. Dinner was between 5:00 p.m. and 5:30 p.m., and we had to be home in time to sit down with the family for dinner, especially when our fathers whistled for us to come home. Every father had his own distinct whistle. My father would hold his pointer and middle fingers between his lips. With his lips slightly closed he would blow a sharp loud whistle meant only for the Gaudi kids. We had five minutes, and we had to be home. I can't remember ever ignoring his whistle.

Ron, Rich, and me

Dinner was the day's most important time and event for most families. Dad was home, Mom had prepared a big meal, and we kids were expected to sit at the dinner table, eat everything on our plates, and be grateful for what we had. Parents worked hard to put food on the table, and they expected mealtime to be family time. Sometimes we didn't like the food (I especially didn't like lima bean soup and liver), but there wasn't a choice. Whatever it was, we had to eat it.

"Home" is the other name I give when my grandkids ask me to name my favorite restaurant. We never went out to eat. My mother cooked every day, and when Dad got home from work we ate exactly at 5:00 p.m. We would sit down together at the dining room table and eat what was put on our plates. My dad always insisted that we sit until we finished our meal. I can vividly remember taking a couple of hours to eat a few of my dinners. I wasn't permitted to leave the dinner table until my plate was clean. After a while, Mom would usually come to my rescue. She would remove my plate and say, "Don't ask for any dessert." Thank God for moms.

The cost of food for an average family in the early fifties was approximately twenty dollars per week. A few examples of food costs during the early 1950s:

- ✧ Apples twenty cents per pound
- ✧ American cheese forty-five cents per pound
- ✧ Bananas thirteen cents per pound
- ✧ Campbell's Tomato Soup ten cents per can
- ✧ Chuck roast fifty-nine cents per pound
- ✧ Coffee thirty-seven cents per pound
- ✧ Family-style loaf of bread twelve cents
- ✧ Hamburger meat thirty cents per pound
- ✧ Juicy oranges thirty-five cents per dozen

✧ Lettuce twelve cents per head

✧ Margarine nineteen cents per pound

✧ Pork and beans eight cents per can

✧ Potatoes seven cents per pound

✧ Sliced bacon thirty-five cents per pound

✧ Sugar eight cents for five pounds

✧ Toilet tissue five cents per roll

I can't remember ever going out to eat in a restaurant with my family, probably because there were six of us and money was scarce. My mom could feed a family at home much cheaper than taking us out to eat. And we weren't the only ones. Most families in High Park just didn't go to restaurants. The first time I ate in a restaurant with linens was when I was a freshman in college.

Lesson #2: Dads and moms who work hard to provide for their families deserve the respect, cooperation, and admiration of their children.

Chapter 2
Electronics & Technology

During my early childhood we didn't have penicillin, polio shots, Xerox copies, contact lenses, credit cards, cell phones, ballpoint pens, or Frisbees. There was no such thing as an FM radio, a tape deck, a compact disc or CD player, a video game, or a personal computer.

We did have telephones though. During this period of time, 1949-54, the telephone was a big black bulky contraption, much different from the telephones of today. Our telephones were all connected on party lines with two different households having the same phone line. Some households had more than two; some had as many as eight parties. When we tried to use the telephone and the other party was using the line, we had to hang up and wait until they were finished. We didn't use the telephone very much because of the sharing. You made your call and kept it brief.

As a pre-schooler, radio was the key home entertainment center. My father on Sunday mornings always listened to the polka station. I do remember listening to the radio in the evening but recall only the *Amos and Andy* comedy show and the *Inner Sanctum* mystery show. As I got older I listened religiously, as did most boys, to the Pittsburgh Pirates baseball games. I remember, even though I was a young boy, walking home through the neighborhood during the summertime and listening to the Pirates ball game because all the neighbors had their windows open (no airconditioning!) and radios tuned to KDKA-AM, which carried the Pittsburgh Pirates. The Pirates were a good, solid ball club, and either you liked Bob Prince the Pirates broadcaster or you hated him. I liked him. Everyone during those days seemed to be a baseball fan.

When my parents bought a television in 1951, that piece of technology changed our lives. The television (TV) held a small, circular screen inside a large, heavy, wooden cabinet called a "console." The TV was always located in the living room, where the whole family could watch together. I believe we were one of the first in the neighborhood to have this new invention.

We thought it was a miracle! It brought news and entertainment into our living room—not just sound but also pictures! It was hard to comprehend that those electronic waves could be sent through the air, caught by an antenna strapped to our chimney, and then turned into a black and white picture with a voice and all kinds of other sounds. For years we had only three stations to watch and the programming didn't come on until mid-afternoon. TV programming signed off at midnight with the playing of our national anthem.

Later in the early 1950s, TV programming expanded to mornings. Saturday mornings for me became the most important time to watch TV. *Sky King, Tarzan, Roy Rogers, Gene Autry, The Lone Ranger, The Three Stooges, Laurel and Hardy,* and cartoons could be seen at this time of the day. This was my time, and I would normally watch two to three hours of TV on most Saturdays, especially during the winter. After I'd seen all my shows, I would get dressed and go outside to play.

Chapter 3

Our "Field of Dreams"

As young kids during all the seasons, WE WERE (almost) ALWAYS OUTSIDE PLAYING! The game of choice depended on the time of the year. In the fall, our favorite pastimes were football, army (similar to hide and seek), and playing in the woods. In spring and summer it was baseball/softball, riding bikes, kick the can, Buckety Buck, and Belt Lily.

Buckety Buck and Belt Lily may not be familiar to people these days. We didn't play these games very often because of the number of players needed and the intensity of the game. We played Buckety Buck like this: a minimum of eight players—four members on each team—would leap one at a time on the arched backs of the opposing players positioned in a row while holding on to each other around his waist. When everyone on the team had completed the jump, an assigned member of the "horse" or arched team attempted to guess the number of fingers on one hand that the opponent was holding up. If he guessed the number correctly, the teams would reverse positions. The game created many sore necks, backs, and ribs!

Belt Lily was a game played with an individual hopping on one leg in a designated area attempting to tag other players. Once tagged, both players would run, with two legs of course, as fast as they could back to the safety line before being smacked on the back side by the other players with a folded belt below the waist—ouch!

Another spontaneous adventure included playing in the woods. The woods were adjacent to our property. We could go south or west and experience Mother Nature's best—woods, green pastures, and streams.

We would walk at least a half mile into the woods. While climbing one of the big trees, we would challenge each other to see who could scale the highest limb. Then we would give a Tarzan call or just yell at the top of our lungs and swing like monkeys in the trees. When we got bored with the trees, we would walk through the wooded area quietly looking for deer, fox, squirrels, and chipmunks. When we came to a stream we would then begin looking for snakes, lizards, or any small creatures that lived along the banks of the creek. Sometimes we would get thirsty and drink the water in the stream. It appeared clean to us. We figured if the cows, deer, and other creatures of the forest can drink the water, why can't we. Fortunately for us, we never got sick—maybe we were just lucky!

Finally, on our journey home we would walk through the cow pastures attempting to harass the cows by chasing them to the other end of the field—unless, of course, the bulls were in the pasture. Then, we would hug the fence line and walk as quietly as possible in order to avoid any interaction with the bull or bulls. They were very unfriendly and had no fear of us.

The High Park kids were fortunate to have an area where we could play on a field, in the woods, or on a road. In fact, we were fortunate to have two separate fields—a baseball field and a football field. Kids today might find these two fields unacceptable because of their conditions. They weren't fancy, they weren't professionally designed, they weren't maintained by a park service, but they were ours, and we considered ourselves lucky to have them. This is where everyone strengthened athletic abilities and developed important character qualities.

Our "field of dreams" wasn't like the fields of today. Left center of the baseball/softball field was a rock quarry; a ground rule double was called when a fly ball or grounder ended up in the rock quarry. Right field had trees beyond the ordinary position of the fielder, but there were no special ground rules for the trees. The entire outfield had tall grass, about a foot in height, in certain areas where at times running for a fly ball could end up with a fielder slipping or tripping and disappearing in the grass. The infield was slanted toward the outfield and was littered with little stones and bumpy clumps of grass. Nobody complained, and few infielders ever attempted to remove the little stones. We learned how to play baseball on that field. We shared our gloves, bats, and balls. We repaired our bats with nails and tape. We learned to catch fly balls and retrieve grounders. We all became above-average ball players.

At seven years of age Jay, my best friend, and I both got drafted to a Little League team in our first-year tryouts. Back then in Little League not everyone who tried out got selected or drafted. The Little League coaches told the kids who didn't get drafted to practice more and come back the following year. What would parents do today if their kids didn't get drafted?

Lesson #3: If you were good, you were selected. If you weren't good, you worked to improve your skills and try again next time.

Chapter 4

Little League

Our Little League field was located at McKee Stadium in Jeannette. This was a great place to play baseball. Jay was drafted and played centerfield for the Knights of Columbus, and I played second base for the Eagles. I played on a good ball club, and Jay was selected to a team that won only a few games his first year. My most memorable moment of that year came during the middle of the season. Our team was beating Jay's Knights of Columbus team 8-0.

In the fifth inning I came to the plate with the bases loaded. I hit a deep, high fly ball to left centerfield. Jay was playing centerfield. He ran over to his right, stretching his arm over the outfield fence and catching what would have been a grand slam home run. It was an unbelievable catch. When he came off the field, all of his teammates cheered him as he approached the bench. I still believe today it was the best catch ever made in the history of Jeannette Little League baseball. He and I still talk about his great catch that one summer day.

Lesson #4: It is possible to enjoy another person's successes as much as our own.

Chapter 5

Stickball, High Park Playground, and De-Pantsing

Jay, my best friend, and I played together just about every day of our summer childhood lives. We made games up like stocking ball and our own version of stickball. Stocking ball was played with a sock stuffed slightly larger than a golf ball with tape wrapped around the outer layer. The ball for stickball was made out of paper (usually newspaper) squeezed into a round circle about the size of a golf ball and then wrapped with tape. We would find an old broom handle approximately three feet in length and play ball for hours in front of his house. Both games were played one-on-one with baseball rules but without the running. We had imaginary lines for a single, double, triple, and home run. A fly ball past the pitcher was a single, a double was beyond the single, and so forth. We would bat right-handed and then at times left-handed, and we played fast-pitch. We developed a sharp eye, and when we started playing Little League baseball, we rarely struck out.

After the High Park School closed, the property was turned into a township playground. The playground had swings, a sliding board, a monkey bar, and a merry-go-round. The schoolhouse was used for indoor board games like Monopoly, Sorry, Dominoes, or Checkers. During the summer this was another place for the High Park kids of all ages to congregate for a good time. One of the major reasons the kids my age would get together was to play on an organized softball team. We had home games on our "Field of Dreams" and away softball games in which we would travel to other playgrounds in the township of Hempfield. We would take every game seriously and each year always won more games than we lost.

When we played a home game, which always began at 6:00 p.m., occasionally a very unusual thing would take place. First of all, a crowd of teenagers and some adults would gather and watch us play. They would cheer for us and encourage us to give our best. We couldn't have asked for anything more from the home crowd.

After the game the teenagers would congratulate us and then their fun began as we became their victims. This didn't happen often, but it happened maybe once, sometimes twice a year. One or more teenagers would holler, "De-pants!" This meant chasing us, catching us, and then taking our pants off and throwing them into the nearby trees, bushes, or worse yet, handing them to a teenage girl. We would run as fast as we could using all our finesse to get away from them, but when three motivated teenagers have decided to run you down for their laughs at your expense, escape was very unlikely.

To say the least, it was embarrassing. After completely humiliating us, they would let us up off the ground so we could search for our pants, hoping that no one would see us. They showed no sympathy. They would all laugh at us and then return to the nearby playground while we attempted to find our pants in the deep shadows of near dark. We never ran home and told our parents about the "de-pantsing" part. We lived with it; it was all part of growing up. I don't remember how this tradition ever started, but it ended when we became teenagers ourselves. Thank God.

Lesson #5: To avoid humiliation after the last inning—win or lose—run home as fast as you can.

Chapter 6

Summer Games: Mumbley Peg, Buckety Buck, Belt Lily, and Kick the Can

For Mumbley Peg, the only equipment needed was a pocketknife. Yes, a pocketknife! The knife usually had one or two blades. At that point in our young lives, it was a necessary tool for cutting things, cleaning grimy fingernails, whittling, or playing Mumbley Peg. Usually the pocketknife was a Christmas or birthday gift. These knives were durable and inexpensive. They were special, and most of the time kids my age didn't carry their knives for fear of losing them.

On a hot summer day, a rainy day, or any time a couple of kids had nothing to do or were just plain bored, we would play Mumbley Peg. Our version of the game required accuracy in our ability to throw a pocketknife. There were few rules and no referees. Like most of our games, we followed the honor system.

The game has many local variations, but we played like this: two, sometimes three, people took their positions. The key to winning was to be able to throw a knife and make it stick in the ground. Two kids stood approximately four to five feet apart facing each other, feet together. The first person would throw a knife, trying to make it land and stick within a foot or less of another player. If the knife landed farther away, the throw would not count. If the knife stuck and was within a foot, the second player would move his foot to the location of the knife. Then it was the other (or next) player's turn to throw the knife. The same rules applied. If the knife's blade didn't stick in the ground or the person threw the knife too far, a player didn't have to move his foot.

The objective of the game was to see who could get the other person to stretch to the point where he would either fall over or not be able to touch his opponent's knife with his foot. There were no ties in this game. Any disputes were settled in typical boy fashion—by yelling. It might be surprising, but I can honestly say I cannot remember any player ever being stuck in the foot or leg with a knife.

Lesson #6: Success, achievement, and improvement require practice, practice, and more practice!

"Buckety Buck" wasn't played very often because a minimum of eight players was needed—four on each team. The two teams consisted of a "horse team" and a "jumping team." First of all, we would pick out a utility pole, a tree, or a sturdy lamppost for the horse team's player who would use it as a back brace. The captains were selected and each picked a team by throwing even or odd numbers with their fingers. One person would say, "One ... two ... three!" On "three," both captains would throw a certain amount of fingers with one hand. If the person called even and the fingers of both persons totaled even, then he had the choice to decide if his team wanted to be the "horse team" or the "jumping team."

The horse team was made up of one person standing upright against a tree, utility pole, or lamp post, and the next kid on the team would arch over, spread his feet for maximum strength and balance, lock arms around the waist of the pole person, and rest his head against the hip of that person. The next team person would position (feet, legs, head, and arms) similar to the person in front of him until all the team players were positioned forming a row of "horses." The other team's players, the leapers, would then take a running jump, one at a time, and each would leap as far as he could without falling to the ground onto the row of "horses." Each member of the jumping team would follow, one by one, until the last person who jumped would holler out, "Buckety Buck, how many fingers up?" The captain of the jumping team would show his hand with the number of fingers to the post person. Then the captain of the horse team, not being the post person, would attempt to guess the number. If he happened to guess the right number, the teams would reverse positions. I can always remember the groans after someone jumped, slamming the weight of his body onto bent backs braced for impact, or being kicked in the side of the ribs or head by a knee from one of the jumpers.

Other rules of the game required a team to reverse its positions if a member of the leaping team fell off the row of any horse. At times players could and would get hurt during this game, particularly when the jumper, instead of leaping on someone's back, landed instead on someone's head or neck. Once in a while a jumper would leap and misjudge his target, potentially hitting a person and the ground at the same time–ouch! It's hard to imagine, but it happened. This game was dangerous as ribs, head, and neck were susceptible to injuries, but, amazingly enough, nothing major happened. Nobody ever broke an arm or leg. It was just a lot of fun with many laughs both during the game and sometimes for days after.

Lesson #7: Some injuries can be avoided by carefully focusing on what we are doing.

"Belt Lily" was also an occassional summer game in our neighborhood. We usually played this game on a level area of a road. Rocks or sticks were used to line off an area approximately fifteen yards wide by fifteen yards in length. Hand numbers were thrown against each other, evens and odds. The players who lost would then match up with the other losers until a "Lily" was chosen. The Lily's objective was to hop on one leg while attempting to touch another person within the designated boundaries and returning to the marked safety zone. A key element of the game was that the "Lily" person could not touch the ground with his non-hopping foot. If the "Lily" accidentally dropped his foot and touched the ground, the other players were permitted to use their belts as a weapon, striking the player on his backside, below the waist, until he crossed into the safety zone.

The best strategy for the "Lily" was to choose a target, tag that person and avoid being whipped below the waistline by the other players before crossing the safety line. Again, once the person hopping on one leg touched another person with his hand, we were free to use both feet to run back, as fast as we could, to the safety line. The other players with their belts folded had open season on your backside until you crossed the safety zone. I remember running scared but fast. At that moment it wasn't fun. Did it hurt? Of course! I remember having tears in my eyes, but actual crying was *not* an option.

> **Lesson #8:** Like life in general, strategy and bravery were the two most important qualities needed in these games.

Another game, "Kick the Can," was a fun summer game. It was usually played after dark. "Kick the Can" was very similar to hide and seek, except a tin can was placed on top of a brick or stone. The person who was "it" had to close his eyes and count to fifty while the other kids hid nearby within a defined area. When the person who was "it" opened his eyes, he would have to find the other kids. Once the "it" person spotted someone, he would touch the can and call his name out to make that player his prisoner. If any kid beat the "it" person to the can, he would kick the can, and the "it" person would have to start the game all over again. All prisoners would go back into hiding. Once the "it" person took everyone prisoner, the first person who was caught would be the "it" person.

The noise of the can being kicked could be heard loud and clear, and the sound brought all the kids out of hiding, talking and laughing about how they were prepared to "kick the can" themselves. Only the porch lights and, at times, the moon would provide enough light to make the game fun. Good players never wandered too far from the "can." We had to learn timing and be honest with ourselves about how fast we could move compared to the other players. Bragging about speed and strategy didn't do any good if it couldn't be backed up on the playing field.

Lesson #9: Controlled speed and an ability to hide can be useful skills to develop and maintain.

Chapter 7
BB Guns and Camping Out

I didn't play much with my brothers Ron and Rich. Ron was five years older and Rich was three years older than I. I had my friends, and they had theirs. I do remember one particular incident with my brother Ron during my younger years when I received a Red Rider BB gun for Christmas. I was about nine years old and was thrilled about being the owner of what I considered at the time to be such a well-crafted and reliable firearm. During the winter I didn't get to shoot it much, but when spring came around I went outside and started to practice.

the gang

My cousin Billy was a year older than I. He lived only about a half mile from us. One day he came to visit and brought his BB gun. We felt so powerful with our weapons. We had a great time shooting at tin cans, glass bottles, and rats in our dump pile, which was located behind our garage where we burned our garbage. We had no garbage pickup in the early fifties. After so many years we would relocate the garbage pit by digging another. That is where I learned about fire and how it could really burn your skin. Guns and fire and freedom gave us a real sense of manly authority and territorial dominance.

We were focused only on how many BBs we could shoot that day. We were having a great time until we ran out of BBs, but I knew where my brother Ron kept his supply. I went into the garage and took a pack from his hidden stockpile. As I was leaving the garage with my loaded BB gun, my brother came running out of the house and asked me if I had taken any of his BBs.

Of course, afraid of my older brother, I denied doing any such thing. I figured there was no way he could know, but he looked at me and could see that I was not telling the truth.

His threat was simple and clear: "If any of my BBs are missing, I am coming after you."

I was scared until Billy said, "Let's hide behind this tree; when he opens the side door of the garage, we'll keep him pinned inside the garage by using our BB guns. Then he will beg *us not to shoot at him anymore and beg for mercy. Then you can forgive him.*"

I thought it was a great idea and agreed—*bad* idea.

When he opened the side door to the garage, we began shooting at him. He immediately closed the door. Billy and I were laughing, and for just a few minutes we were not worrying about any consequences. We had control of the situation.

Everything was going as planned until Billy realized he was getting low on BBs. He decided to bolt from my yard and went running up the road as fast as his legs could carry him toward his home, leaving me there all alone. By that time, Ron had opened the garage door with his BB gun in hand, and he was mad as you know what. At that moment, I knew the circumstances had changed. My gut feeling told me to run, so I took off as fast as I could toward the woods to get away from my brother, who saw that I was leaving the crime scene. He began the chase, and I heard him yelling that he was going to shoot me. I believed him, so my desperate goal was to reach the woods and somehow disappear. I started my mad dash down the steep slope of the terrain. When I happened to come upon a large rock with a big overhang, I quickly decided to climb under the rock to hide with the hope that my brother would never find me; I felt secure and closed my eyes.

Moments later I heard my brother walking near my perfect hiding place. I told myself he wouldn't find me and kept my eyes closed tight. But within a few seconds I felt the barrel of his BB gun in my back. Afraid of being shot, I kicked up with my legs and hit my brother's hand causing the BB gun to discharge into my back. That's when I felt this very sharp pain. Ron had inadvertently pulled the trigger. The pain was terrible. I climbed out from beneath the rock screaming and crying. My brother calmly explained, "I really wasn't going to shoot you." I had a white T-shirt on, and it immediately began showing blood. My brother took my shirt off and inspected the damage. I was still crying loudly. He saw the wound and said he was sorry. Then I saw the worried look on his face and heard him say, "Please don't tell Dad!"

The pain was awful, but after a few minutes I stopped crying and promised him I wouldn't tell anyone. We went home, and he treated the injury with Merthiolate. Boy did that burn. The pain lasted into the night and beyond. I remember sleeping on my stomach for the next several nights. I never mentioned a word to my mother or father. But from that day forward my brother Ron and I became a little closer as brothers.

Lesson #10: Apologies don't have power to heal wounds, but they can heal relationships.

In those years, once or twice a summer I would invite one of my friends to camp out in my family's large backyard. It was a great spot for braving the elements and stargazing. Our arrangements included a blanket and some food—usually sandwiches and cookies. We would get water from the spigot in our garage and use our canteens for our water supply. We would lie on our blankets looking at the stars, watching airplanes, and at times watching for meteors, but we called them "shooting stars." Sometimes we would claim that we saw alien spaceships flying over us. We would finally fall asleep talking kid stuff. Usually we would sleep only for a few hours before waking up because of the chill and dampness of the night. Eventually we would move to my front porch. There we would sleep on the glider or couch until daylight. We didn't do this very often, but we cherished the moments of those special nights under the stars.

> **Lesson #11:** Not only are life's simple pleasures often the most memorable and satisfying, they are also often the least expensive.

Chapter 8

Summer Job: Caddying

The summer I turned nine years old, my brothers took me to Baldock Hills Country Club. Baldock Hills CC was a country club where young kids like me could earn money caddying. In those days there were very few places for kids my age to earn a buck. If I caddied nine holes with a single golf bag, I would receive one dollar and fifty cents, which included a twenty-five-cent tip. For players who went eighteen holes, the fee would double to three dollars including tip. At that time, three dollars for four hours of work was great income for a young man. I needed money for my personal needs—school clothes, movie theatre tickets, treats, and gadgets of all kinds. When caddying, golfers who lost a golf ball in play—on the golf course—usually would *not* give a tip. We were expected to find every ball that stayed in play. So we kept a sharp eye on the golf ball and used any marker—trees, shrubs, rocks, any course feature—to locate the ball. We did not want to lose that tip.

I will never forget the caddie master, Adolph. He would take ten cents per bag for every eighteen holes caddied. If we made three dollars, he would take ten cents. Today we would call it a "kickback." By mid-summer my friend Jay became interested in earning money, so he began to caddy too. Later that summer my friends from High Park, Don and Ron, began to caddy. Why? Because we all needed money.

How did we get back and forth from Baldock Hills CC every day? Believe it or not, we hitchhiked every day to and from the club. We would walk from home approximately one mile to the main highway, Route 30. From there we would hitchhike to the golf course. The total distance was approximately five miles from our house. Some days it could take a few minutes to catch a ride, and other days it could take as long as an hour.

Why didn't someone drive us to the golf course? The main reason was our parents had only one car and our fathers would drive to work, and our mothers didn't drive. We never had a problem with any individual who picked us up. They were always courteous. I caddied eight years at Baldock Hills CC. Can you imagine? No one should try hitchhiking today—especially children!

I do have a vivid memory of a summer afternoon after Jay and I had finished caddying a full round of eighteen holes. We walked from the club to the main highway, which was about one hundred and fifty yards from the parking lot of the country club, to begin our traditional hitchhiking journey home. It was one of those hot August days when it seemed that nobody was interested in picking up two young kids. I was doing the hitching that day, and Jay was sitting in the grass. That's how we did it in those days.

Finally, after standing there for at least a half hour, Jay commented that I was too ugly to fetch us a ride, and he volunteered to trade places for a while. He also proclaimed that I wasn't extending my arm and thumb out far enough. Within moments a car began to slow down, and Jay excitedly claimed he'd been right about my looks, when suddenly a hand launched a large cup out the window. Abruptly Jay got showered with a creamy mess. It turned out to be a vanilla milk shake. The words that came from Jay's mouth in that moment I can't repeat in this book. I laughed so hard tears were running down my face. I do recall hearing the two teenagers drive off, laughing loudly. We found a piece of cloth in the grass and attempted to wipe the milk shake off of Jay's face and clothes. We weren't completely successful. Yes, we finally got a ride. When we got into the car of the person who picked us up, he asked Jay what happened. I gave him the full details of the event. The person never laughed out loud, but he had a smile on his face the whole way home.

Lesson #12: Some chances are worth taking, but all choices have consequences.

One summer morning a few weeks later, Jay and I were standing on the tee of the fourth hole of the golf course with steady hands on our players' golf bags. At that age, we were permitted to carry only a single golf bag because we lacked experience and strength to handle two. Because of the narrow tee, we were but a few feet in front of the tee and standing approximately eight feet from the golfers. The golfers we were caddying for were not the best players we'd ever seen. My golfer placed his ball on the tee, took a big swing, and hit the ball down the fairway approximately 210 yards. Jay's golfer told my player, "Good shot." They both agreed. Jay and I both concurred by saying, "Great drive" simultaneously. As a caddy, those were the things you were supposed to say to make your golfer feel good.

Jay's golfer approached the tee box, put his tee in the ground, and placed his ball on top of the tee. He lined up his shot and proceeded to take a big swing, and within a split second the golf ball sliced and hit Jay in the face. He immediately fell to the ground. Both golfers quickly approached to see if he was injured. Jay got up immediately, claiming that he was OK. Both of our golfers checked him over. When Jay finally looked over to me, I began to smile. Why? Because Jay's right cheek was red and swollen and had dimpled impressions from the impact of the golf ball. As we began walking up the fairway, the golfers again asked Jay if he was OK. And again he said he was fine. Our group finally finished golfing eighteen holes. The mark on Jay's cheek was still easy to see. Because of that incident, both golfers gave us two dollars for a tip—the most we ever received as single-carrying caddies.

Why did Jay say he was OK? If he had gotten hurt while he was caddying, Adolph the caddie master would have *never* let him caddy again at the country club.

Lesson #13: Never bite the hand that feeds you.

Among other memorable incidents, another event took place on the golf course that I will never forget. I was caddying in the club championship event. My club member was playing match play. In match play, whoever shoots the lowest score on the hole wins the hole. If players tie, no one wins the hole. My player was three up on his opponent with four holes to play. Our opponent hit a misdirected second shot over the green on the fifteenth hole. My member hit his second shot perfectly onto the green of that difficult hole, and that meant he would be putting for a birdie. We both knew if we beat our opponent on this hole the match was over. At that moment, I was thinking about getting a big tip from my golfer. Then it happened. As we both walked together up the slight grade of the hill to the green and were talking about his great golfing performance that day, my member suddenly collapsed. On the ground and in pain, he was gasping for air. Within seconds his face turned red and blue. Our opponent and other nearby members gathered around him to assist in some way, but nobody knew CPR. There was no medical doctor nearby that day. At the direction of these adults, I ran as fast as I could back to the clubhouse and reported the incident to the caddy master, who notified an ambulance service. Unfortunately, by the time the ambulance reached the site, the member had expired. I found out later my golfer had suffered a massive heart attack.

Lesson #14: Life is unpredictable, so never assume anything.

Chapter 9

The Rat Story

I recall one sunny summer day Jay and I were playing a game of stickball in front of his house when I noticed something across the street moving in the sewer pipe. At first it appeared to be a big muskrat. I quietly called to Jay and told him to look across the street into the sewer pipe. As we stared at the critter, we immediately realized it was a "big fat rat." As we approached the sewer pipe slowly and carefully, the rat stared at us, acknowledging our presence, and then he disappeared into the pipe. At that moment, our hearts were beating one hundred miles per hour, our eyes were as big as baseballs, plus we were both experiencing an adrenalin rush, and, to be honest, we were also scared out of our wits.

We both decided we wanted to catch the rat, but how? My oldest brother Ron was a trapper and had equipment to catch many different types of animals. I decided to run home and borrow one. When I returned we strategically placed the trap in the sewer line and spread some peanut butter on the spring-loaded tongue of the trap. We then decided to go into the house so as not to disrupt our strategy and played a game of cards.

About a half hour later, we came back outside and found to our surprise that we had caught the rat in our trap. It was still alive and squirming. Jay and I found two sticks and beat the rat until it didn't move. We were both still cautious about the varmint. We waited a few minutes, but finally I cautiously picked up the chain attached to the trap, and the rat did not move. It was dead.

We were so proud of our achievement that we wanted to show Mrs. Parks, our neighbor, what we had caught in her sewer pipe. With satisfied smiles on our faces, we knocked on her front door, Mrs. Parks answered, and we raised the "big fat rat" up to her face for a good, close look. Before we could say anything else, she let out a *scream* that carried a mile in all directions! She quickly slammed the front door on us. Disappointed and confused, we slowly walked across the street to Jay's house with the rat hanging from the trap. But before we got to Jay's yard—news traveled fast with moms—his mom came racing outside the house questioning us about scaring Mrs. Parks with a dead animal.

Then she noticed what we were carrying. We were approximately ten yards from Jay's mom when she identified the monster. She asked us not to come any closer. All she wanted was answers. We told her the whole story. By then Mrs. Parks was standing on her porch, still shaken; Jay's mom approached her and explained to her how that "big fat rat" was caught in the sewer pipe in front of Mrs. Parks's house. She began to calm down. Then both expressed their gratitude by rewarding us with a twenty-five-cent bounty with a caveat that we bury the "big fat rat" in the woods immediately. We didn't waste any time. We went straight to the woods.

Following the burial, Jay and I immediately went to Tony's Store—a little convenience store located on Baughman Avenue in High Park. We purchased a candy bar, a Popsicle, and a pop (soda), and still had money left over. Wow!! As we sat on the edge of the walkway eating and drinking our goodies, we told our story to anyone who would listen as they approached us at the store. We were so proud of ourselves. On that particular day, we were heroes to the mothers on Cort Street.

Lesson #15: Mothers (in every generation) hate rats.

Chapter 10

Smoking

During the early fifties, almost all male adults smoked cigarettes, cigars, or pipes, or chewed tobacco. I remember that I started smoking when I was in second grade. Yes, only seven years old. On selected summer Sundays after church, members of the M&S Club (an Italian club which stood for "married & single") would have stag parties. The M&S "Men's" Club was located a few hundred yards beyond our house in the woods. They would eat, drink, smoke, and play games, cards, Mooda (an Italian numbers game), Bocce, and just have a good old time.

On most Monday mornings my friends and I would visit the M&S Club site and pick up cigarette butts and half-smoked cigars. We would use our penknives to cut both ends off of the cigars and cigarettes. We figured we had sanitized them. Then we would sit in the woods for a couple of hours smoking up a storm. At times we would try to inhale, but that would bring on a coughing spell. When we finished smoking, we would place our leftover cigarettes and cigars into a tin can and bury them until we had another opportunity to smoke again. We did this most of that summer.

One day I even bought a pack of cigarettes (Lucky Strike) for nineteen cents. This came from a double dare by my friends. The money came from three of us—a total of twenty cents. (By the way, I kept the penny.) I told the lady who owned the store that it was for my father. She looked at me, and I convinced her by saying, "Honest!" She believed me, or at least she acted like she did. Later that day, the three of us smoked the pack of cigarettes.

By late August I came down with a terrible cough. By happenstance, my mother was going to the doctor's that week and explained to Doctor Naples, our family doctor, my symptoms. The doctor asked my mother if I was smoking. My mother was shocked by the idea and replied that I was only seven years old. The doctor said, "I didn't ask you how old your son was; I asked you if your son smoked."

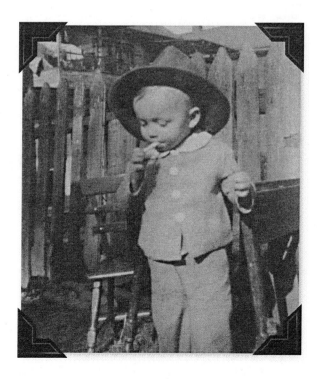

Later, when she arrived home, my mother interrogated me about whether or not I was using tobacco. I denied it completely. She said that the doctor thought my cough might be caused from smoking cigarettes. She said the doctor wanted to see me if the cough persisted. If my parents had found out that I was smoking, the consequences would have been severe. Well, needless to say, I quit smoking that day, and my cough gradually went away. To this day, I have never smoked another cigarette.

Lesson #16: Smoking is dangerous to your health and causes coughing (among other bad things).

Chapter 11

Play: Fall Football, Army Maneuvers, and Cow Riding

Today, I believe kids play more indoors than outdoors because of all the fancy gadgets and toys. But when they do participate in outside activities—such as football, soccer, baseball, and hockey—they are usually organized with adult supervision.

During September, October, and November when we played outdoors after school, we usually played on our football field located about two hundred yards below the baseball field. Tino Bertolino's parents owned this piece of property and rarely complained about our activities. Our football field was about thirty yards in length and twenty yards wide, and the rest of the field was covered with short trees, tall grass, and thorny bushes. We used the tall grass and thorny bush section of the field to play army (one of our favorite versions of hide-and-seek).

The football field was slightly slanted east to west with small potholes and the occasional rock protruding slightly out of the ground. We had only one good football, and it belonged to Jay—a very welcome Christmas gift. Of course all of our games were unsupervised. We kids honed our catching, tackling, blocking, and running skills on that field. At times we would go home after a pick-up football game looking like we had been dragged through the mud. As we walked home, the game would be replayed (with the occasional embellishment "protruding slightly" out of the facts) as we reminisced about great catches, passes, or tackles made on those near-perfect autumn days.

Also during this time of the year we would play Army in the lower section, where the tall grass and bushes were located. Army was played like a hide-and-seek game. Teams were chosen, and one group would count to fifty while the other side hid in the field. The object was to crawl through the tall grass and under the short bushes without being seen while searching carefully for opposing team members. In other words, both teams' members were hunting each other. We used sticks as rifles. It was a very quiet game until someone spotted one of the opposing members in the grass and pretended to shoot them: "Bang, bang!" or "Rat-tat-tat!" The person "shot" was eliminated from the game. He would leave the field and stand in the open part of the field. The person who shot him would again immediately go back into hiding—back to hunting.

Sometimes an argument would pursue because opposing players claimed they had shot the other. The rule? Both dead. Out of the game for that round. The winning team had to eliminate all the players from the other team. Sometimes as many as three or four people could be hunting for just one of their "enemies." It was a game of patience and stealth combined with strategy. Our army exercises could last a good half hour or so, and it was always fun to play.

Lesson #17: Patience, strategy, and teamwork are keys to success!

Occasionally in the early fall before the real hunting season began, my friends and I would go into the neighboring woods of High Park with our BB guns. We would practice target shooting at objects such as cans, rocks, and trees as we walked through the woods. But on one particular day, we came upon some cows meandering in a pasture near a crab apple tree. I clearly remember this particular Saturday afternoon. That morning I had just finished watching a bronco-riding cowboy movie. I came up with the bright idea that we should attempt to bronco ride a cow. While walking through a pasture with cows grazing that afternoon, I explained this idea to my friends. My idea turned into a "double dare" from them for me to go first. A double dare in those days was like calling someone a chicken, and you would be scarred for life if you didn't follow through with the dare. I could feel my blood go cold as I climbed the crab apple tree and prepared to carry out my cowboy feat. Was there fear in my heart? Of course!

I was hoping they wouldn't be able to move the cows under the tree, but finally they managed to position a cow beneath my perch. It took great courage and stupidity on my part, but I did it.

I jumped. It happened so quickly. I dropped approximately four feet onto the back of an unsuspecting cow. The surprised animal let out a big "Moooo," took just a few steps, then bucked me high into the air. I landed on my side in the grassy field, stunned. As I regained my composure, I was worried that the cow was going to chase me, but at the same time I heard laughter and cheers coming from my buddies.

As they ran towards me to see if I was OK, I heard them saying how they couldn't believe what I had just done. I began to feel like a hero. Then I said quickly, as I rose to my feet, "Who's going next?" Nobody volunteered. They all expressed fear about what could happen if a cow stepped on them or bit them, or they fell and broke an arm or leg. As we walked home, all they talked about was my bravery. I do remember the sun was a little bit brighter that day.

Lesson #18: Fear must be faced before courage can be experienced.

Chapter 12

Winter Sledding

In wintertime (December, January, and February), we went sled riding, had snowball fights, and when absolutely necessary, occasionally played indoors. The nice thing about growing up in our neighborhood during the snowy winter days was having a safe place to sled ride: an alley next to our house. It was THE place to sled ride because there was a slight grade in the road making it perfect for kids our age. The alley course was approximately seventy yards long. Another advantage to that alley back then: the High Park community had no sewer system in those days. The ditch in the alley would freeze, causing an overflow of water from the kitchen sinks, washing machines, and other house usages to spill onto the road and turn to ice. The water overflow into the alley provided the best sled riding conditions anywhere. There were only a few neighbors who drove through the alley during the winter, so we had minimal interference from car traffic, and any car tracks were good for sledding.

All the kids and some local teenagers in the community would come to the alley to test their sleds to see who had the fastest. Everyone would line up on an imaginary starting line at the top of the alley. Someone would count to three, and all of us would run as fast as we could with sled in hand, then slam our sleds to the ground while jumping on. The goal was to see who could get to the bottom of the alley first. Wrecks were frequent, and it was always funny to see someone else get upended. We would be up and down that incline over and over until someone would call it quits. Then we would get to the serious part of sledding.

We played a game we called "Bump Off." A "volunteer" would sled down the alley and be chased by the other sledders. We were to count, "1001, 1002, 1003 ...," and chase after him. But we would always cut the count short to 1001, 1002/3 and begin the chase. The objective for the other sledders was to catch that person and bump him off his sled before he could reach the bottom of the alley.

The trick was grabbing the back of the volunteer's sled and pushing the exposed back blade right or left, causing the person steering the sled to lose control and flip over. At times, this meant that sleds would end up off the road and in the drainage ditch. Occasionally we would come up very wet and smelling like sewage. Once in a while, no one would be able to catch the front-runner, and upon arriving at the end of the alley he would jump from his sled, hands in air, claiming victory.

We had lots of laughs. Some kids would get bruised, but they were fun, worthwhile bruises, much different from usual injuries. Everyone would take a turn being a volunteer.

Another favorite winter sledding pastime would be to "double team" on the sled—like bobsledding. Again volunteers would be needed, and eventually everyone took a turn. The double team included a "driver" and "pusher." The driver would position himself with his feet on the glider while sitting on the sled. The pusher would place his hands on the shoulders of his driver and push the sled. After gathering maximum speed, he would jump on back of the sled with his knees resting on the frame and his hands on the shoulder of his partner. Their goal was to ward off or defend any attempt of other bobsledders to upend their sled. Of course the other teams' goal was to cause the person steering the sled to lose control and flip over. Sleds would tumble off into the ditch or roll on the icy track with bodies flying everywhere. At times the pusher or the upright person would sacrifice himself and leap onto the other sledders, knocking them off the track, and rewarding his teammate to claim an infrequent victory. Lots of excitement, laughter, and chatter would follow these incidents. Rarely did a "double team" make it to the bottom of the alley.

We would howl and scream while racing down that alley; probably today someone would call the police or have the alley salted.

Lesson #19: Persevere against the odds …
and have fun doing it!

At Christmastime, it never failed that someone in the neighborhood would get a new sled and want to show it off. Everyone would marvel at the new equipment, wanting to try it out on the track. Brand new, it was clean, shiny, and had gliders that worked. That is, gliders that could easily turn left or right. Every new sled looked like the fastest thing in the world. The older sleds, because of the sledding wars and battles, had cracked wooden frames and damaged gliders from previous crashes. In fact, the red paint on my sled was almost completely rubbed, scraped, and otherwise worn off. All the older neighborhood sleds had battle fatigue and battle scars, evidence of good winter fun.

Here are a few secrets to speeding up a sled:

Sandpaper the steel blades.

Apply wax (candle wax helped me get the maximum speed from my sled).

These were secrets that nobody shared at the time but I learned later that we all knew. Most kids during this era had the name "Lightning Glider" written on the top boards of their sleds. Lightning Glider sleds had a great reputation for speed.

Snowball battles were another winter pastime. If the snow conditions were right, someone would throw a single snowball and an all-out snowball battle would quickly ensue. It would last only a few minutes, often ending as quickly as it began.

After a winter day's snowy fun, we always walked home slowly so we had time to retell each other our tales of the day's funniest and most glorious moments. We parted by simply saying, "See you tomorrow."

Today when I see winter snow or watch someone sled riding down a hill, my memories always rush back to the fun days of sledding in the alley at High Park.

Lesson #20: Bumps, bruises, and scrapes can heal in a few days, but the memories made in the rough and tumble of outdoor play can last a lifetime—priceless life experiences!

Chapter 13

Winter Indoor Games: Table Football and Darts

When it was too cold or inconvenient to go outside, we would usually play indoors at my house or the home of one of my friends.

We played table football on his kitchen table, and we needed only two players and a carefully folded—into a tight triangle—piece of paper for the football. The "pointing" or "middle" fingers were used to strike and slide the football across the table to the other end. If any part of the football was hanging over the edge of the table, a touchdown was scored. To get the extra point, the opposition would make a goalpost by pointing his thumbs up with the index fingers touching and parallel to the table. From about three feet back we would flick or kick the football. One finger would hold the football end up while the other hand's pointer or middle finger would flick the football, sending the ball flying between the goalposts. We used to play this game for hours.

Other winter games included playing with my electric football game or Santa-delivered horse racing games. The electric games during this era were not much fun. Why? Because the football players and race horses wouldn't move in the direction you wanted them to go. That got frustrating fast! Frequently the players or horses would go in the opposite direction or move in a circle—no matter how much we yelled for them to shape up and play right. Sometimes, if we were lucky, the players and horses went where we wanted them to go—much to our pleasure and excitement. We cheered for our players to score a TD or for a certain horse to win. The electric games technology of that era was not the best, but they were games that filled up our afternoons.

One wintry day our friend Denny Parks, who lived directly across the street from Jay, was invited over during the Christmas holiday to play at Jay's house. Even though Denny was slightly younger than we were, he was a good athlete for his age, so we enjoyed including him in our fun.

Jay received a dartboard game from Santa—with real metal darts. Just like the dart game we can see today in some restaurants or local taverns (we used to call them "beer joints"). We were only about nine years old. The last thing Jay's mother said to us as we were racing down the steps into the basement was, "Be careful with those darts." This was a disaster waiting to happen. We hurried down the stairs, loudly claiming first chance to throw the darts. Jay and I established the rules because Denny was too young to argue with us. Of course no one knew any dart rules. But, hey, we had two sets totaling six metal darts, so it wasn't hard to make up our own games.

Here were our rules:

Rule #1—Jay and I would go first.

Rule #2—The third party, Denny, would retrieve the darts until a winner was decided. We agreed that the loser of the game would then be the dart retriever, and the dart retriever would then take on the winner. The third player (whoever was "off" for that round) would become responsible for taking the darts out of the dartboard and handing them over to the players who were throwing the darts.

Rule #3—A person would get one point for hitting the dartboard.

Rule #4—Five points were awarded when a player hit the center of the bull's eye.

Rule #5—Twenty-one points won the game.

About twenty minutes into our impromptu dart game tournament (and having a great time), Jay and I were again competing against each other. Denny, of course, was our retriever. The game became intense, and the competitiveness was at a high pitch. The game was tied at eighteen each. I went first and threw my darts. Two landed on the board, one missed; my score was up to twenty. Then it was Jay's turn. Jay's first dart hit the dartboard. His second dart also hit and stuck to the board. But as he prepared to throw his third dart (for the win), his first dart came loose and fell to the basement floor.

An argument ensued as to how long a dart had to remain stuck on the board before it became a point. The pitch of our argument rose because the game was close. I knew if his dart counted, he then had twenty points and could win the game with his last throw. So I had to protect myself against losing. Jay and I continued to argue about the fallen dart while Denny went over to the board to pick up the dart off the floor. There was only one problem in all of this: Denny didn't realize Jay had one more dart left. He thought all the darts were thrown.

While Denny was removing the darts from the board, Jay and I continued to disagree. Jay then decided to throw his last dart without paying attention to his surroundings, including the board. Jay threw his last dart, and it ended up in the side of Denny's neck. Yes, really, right in his neck.

Denny screamed like a wounded cat. The dart was stuck deep in Denny's neck; he wouldn't stop moving so that we could pull the dart out. Blood began to flow, and my first thought was, "Boy, are we in trouble." Finally Denny succeeded in pulling the dart from his own neck. Jay begged him not to cry out loud. He did not want his mother to find out what he had done. He knew he would be punished severely, and none of us would be able to play darts ever again.

Denny did finally settle down with only whimpers and tears. We found an old cloth on his dad's workbench and held it to Denny's neck. That's when Jay and I started to blame each other for what had gone wrong. Finally, Jay did accept responsibility but blamed Denny for not knowing he had another dart to throw. After everything quieted down, we all agreed to keep it a secret for fear of punishment.

Denny went home that evening, and Jay and I were led to believe we had dodged a very large bullet. But early the next morning Denny's mother called Jay's mom about the incident, and all hell broke loose in the Kolinsky house. To say the least, we never played darts again at Jay's house. And I never knew exactly what punishment Jay received, but I believe his Polish father handled it the old-fashioned way—with the belt!

A few years later Denny's family moved. His family was the only family I can remember that ever moved away from High Park.

Lesson #21: Never try to cover up a misdeed by not telling your mother! It's always best to face the truth—and the consequences—of our actions.

Chapter 14

Pinochle

As previously noted, Jay Kolinsky's home was convenient, and his parents were more tolerant than most. So that was the main reason Jay's home was "the place" to play on a rainy or a cold winter day.

Jay's father built their house. He was a self-taught carpenter by trade but worked at the Jeannette Glass Plant. Their home was a one-story, two-bedroom house with a large living room and small kitchen. It also included a full basement. I recall that Jay's home had a coal furnace and was always cozy and warm.

My parents had an older home that was built at the turn of the twentieth century. Our home had two floors and was heated with natural gas. The natural gas space heater was located in the dining room and heated the entire house. The heat was transferred to the upstairs through two ceiling vents that heated three small bedrooms. Our house was small, as were most homes in High Park. We had a basement crawlspace about four feet high until a few years later when my father and brothers dug out the basement to a height of seven feet so we could stand up straight.

Playing cards was something Jay's parents enjoyed doing with us. So at an early age his mother taught us how to play pinochle.

We would play this card game for hours. Sometimes our fourth player was Perry Andiorio, a friend our age, who lived just a few doors down the street from the Kolinskies. We learned how to play competitively at a very early age. As we grew older, it became one of our best Thanksgiving and Christmas evening traditions. Jay and I would always play as partners against his parents, who were both very good pinochle players. We all looked forward to our marathon matches. The games were usually very noisy, funny, and competitive. We continued to play over the next forty-plus years until his mother passed away in late 1980s.

Lesson #22: Learning to play games well can also help a person learn how to make and keep good friends.

Chapter 15

Dogs and Hunting

The majority of the men in High Park hunted small game, mostly rabbits and pheasants, and most hunted with dogs. The south side of High Park was located on the edge of woods, while the southwest fields provided easy access for hunting small game.

After dinner any table scraps, including bones and fat, were given to my dad's hunting dog, which was kept on the other side of our detached two-car garage. My father purposely put the doghouse in view of our kitchen window so he could observe its daily activity. The dog ran on a chain line that extended about ten or fifteen yards. At that point in my life, my job every evening after supper was to feed the dog.

There was only one problem: when I approached the dog with his food in hand, he would get excited, start barking, and jump on me. His sharp nails would dig into my skin and sometimes tear my clothing. On occasion I would try to use strategy and talk to the dog calmly so he would settle down. It never worked. Anyone who came near him with food was a welcome sight, and he just couldn't control himself. The dog was always glad for food and for the company. Once in a while, I would throw the food scraps near his pan to avoid his "harassment." But one day my father observed me using that shortcut. When I came back into the house, he asked me if I had put the food scraps into the dog's dish. With fear running through my veins, I claimed, "Yes." Little did I know that he had been watching me, so the belt came off, and I got a "whipping" I would never forget. It never happened again.

Lesson #23: Never lie to Dad.

My dad and older brothers Ron and Rich loved to hunt. Small game season was a big event in our family, as it was in the majority of High Park families. In preparation for the first day of the season, licenses were purchased, guns were cleaned, clothes and boots were checked and laid out for the big occasion. I'm not sure what my dad did, but he always checked the dog to be sure it was ready. By 7:00 a.m. on the first day of hunting season, morning shots rang out everywhere in the fields and woods surrounding us. It sounded almost like a small army firing its weapons. My father and brothers were good hunters and always brought home their share of rabbits and pheasants. They would lay them out on the ground and talk about their achievements. My mother and I were responsible for cleaning the game for family dinners.

My dad in his lifetime had numerous hunting dogs. Some of the names I remember were Lucky, Lady, King, Queen, and Prince—always a lofty name. On the first day of small game hunting season, he always took his hunting dog into the fields on a leash and then turned it loose and told it to hunt. You must remember the dog was penned up for eleven months, three weeks, and six days out of the year, but my dad expected and demanded that it listen to his every command.

The few times I hunted with my father, his dog would want to run, jump and play, *not* hunt. I could understand why, but I don't believe my father ever did. The dog was just happy to be loose. Dad would get so frustrated with his dogs and would yell commands at them. He would shout with a strong voice at the animals, but they wouldn't listen. Dad would really get frustrated. In these situations, my brothers and I knew better than to say anything to antagonize my father. Season after season, Dad's "hunting" dog would stray off, forcing my dad to give chase. There were times when it seemed like he hunted for his dogs more than they hunted with or for him! After a while, the dog would just disappear into the local woods or fields. We were never sure where these dogs went, but, for whatever reason, they usually returned home later, though some never did.

I can remember my dad saying the most unpleasant things. Then he would look at me. I knew what it meant. At this point, being the youngest, I became the hunting dog. My brothers would smile because they knew what Dad expected of me. I became responsible for walking into the heavy brush, bushes, and cornfields to flush the game out towards my father and brothers so they could shoot.

I rarely got to shoot my shotgun while hunting with my family. But I did one day with my brother Rich. We were hunting together early one autumn Saturday when we came upon a barbed wire fence. We were headed into the next field, and that fence was in our way. My brother went over first and made it just fine. Then it was my turn. Before I began, my brother asked me if my single twelve-gauge shotgun was on safety. I told him it was, *but it wasn't*, and I knew it wasn't. Why? I never got to shoot my gun first because my brothers always were faster than I was getting off the first shot.

For this reason, I decided to be ready if a rabbit or pheasant ever jumped out in front of us. I wanted to shoot first. I started to climb over the fence, and it happened. With my gun in hand, my boot slipped on the barbed wire fence, and my hand accidentally touched the trigger. The gun went off. My brother was approximately ten feet from me. The buckshot blew within a few feet of his face—a near tragedy! It was the scariest thing that ever happened to me.

Lesson #24: Sometimes life gives us second chances.

Before I could get completely over the fence, my brother pulled me head first onto the ground and beat "the living crap" out of me. He never told my dad, thank God. He knew what would have happened. I had plenty to thank God for that day: for the fact that I had not killed my brother and for my brother not telling my father of the incident. I realized a terrible thing could have happened that day because of my stupidity.

Even to this day, my brother Rich and I have never talked about that incident, maybe because we both want to avoid thinking about what could have happened.

> **Lesson #25:** Guns must be handled safely and responsibly and only with the greatest respect for their function.

Chapter 16

My Dog Skippy

Only one of our dogs was ever an actual pet: a mutt named "Skippy." His coat was coal black. He was a special companion and friend to me for three years. Skippy was a dog that understood most commands. He went everywhere with me, of course within the boundaries of High Park. He would even show up when I didn't want him to. I know he just wanted to be with me. Every kid in the neighborhood, including the older teenagers, knew Skippy.

During my two years attending elementary school in High Park, Skippy most days would walk with me the three blocks from my house to the school. Some days when he didn't feel like it or the weather was bad, he would just look at me with his eyes telling me to go it alone. When school let out, he would usually be there waiting to walk me home.

Skippy was a loving mutt who liked to play. He loved the game of baseball. Between innings, if a ball glove ended up on the ground, Skippy would pick it up in his mouth and dare us to catch him. At times he could have three or four kids chasing him around the ball field attempting to retrieve a glove, and he loved it. Skippy was too quick for all of us. More than once he delayed a game for several minutes. I would have to eventually intervene and coax Skippy to hand the glove over to me. He would comply most of the time.

He wasn't welcome on the ball field, and he wasn't welcome in the house at bedtime. Skippy was banned from sleeping upstairs in the bedrooms—my parents' rule. But every morning he would greet me with a wag of his tail, and his eyes would say, "I missed you." We always made the most of the time we got to spend together.

Lesson #26: We can make new friends, but good friends can never be replaced, even when they are "only" pets.

Skippy lived a happy life until one day he came home with a large wound on the back of his neck. We didn't have the money to take him to the veterinarian. My father told me he believed Skippy was shot. We cleaned the wound as best as we could, but within a few weeks, the wound became infected, and Skippy died. I cried for days. I was heartbroken. Skippy lived a short but good life. He was friendly to everyone and trusted everyone. Maybe that's what cost him his life. When he died, I lost one of my best friends and a loyal companion. I buried him near a special tree in our backyard where we used to lie and relax in the heat of summer days. To this day, I have never owned another dog.

Lesson #27: Broken hearts give us strength, understanding, and compassion.

Chapter 17

Automobiles: Travels, Road Conditions, and the Importance of Getting a Good Seat in a Car

Vacations in our neighborhood meant going to a nearby relative's house for a short visit. Once we drove to West Virginia to visit my mother's brother's family for a long weekend. It was a fun visit, but I was glad to return home to my friends. It was rare to ride in a car for pleasure. Cars were used strictly for necessity, and children in our community walked everywhere—to the playground, church, school, store, movies, etc.

Dads drove to work and on the weekends took their wives grocery shopping. Basically we didn't use the car for anything else even though gasoline only cost approximately fifteen cents per gallon. In the early fifties, there were no car seats, booster seats, seat belts, or air bags. And *no one* had air-conditioning!

I remember my first ride in a neighbor's car. It was with my friend's parents, the Kolinskies. I was so excited. I was no more than seven years old. I was invited to go with Jay and his parents to visit his grandparents, who lived a few miles away. I didn't have to tell my parents because his mom told me we would be back before suppertime. Can you believe that? Today parents want to know exactly where their kids are every minute of the day.

Even during this era, all children were required to sit in the back seat of a car—not because of a federal or state law but because the front seat was for "adults only." I recall that Jay raced to the car, opened the rear door on the passenger side, and climbed in. So I followed suit. I ran to the other side of the car and climbed in behind the driver—his father, of course. Jay's father started the car's engine and slowly backed out of his driveway. Because of the dirt roads, a slight dust stirred up as we picked up speed from Cort Street to Pine Street, traveling up a continuous grade until we reached Baughman Avenue, a paved road.

I thought I was a big shot going somewhere—anywhere. We were giggling and just happy to be together. When we got onto the four-lane highway, Route 30, we began to catch the rushing air flowing around us. All of the windows were down! It was a hot summer day, and the breeze felt great.

All of a sudden, I heard a noise coming from Jay's father, and, to my surprise, something hit me in my face. I never saw it coming. I wiped my face and looked at brown sticky liquid on my hand. Jay was laughing light-heartedly, and I began to laugh, too, until I figured it out. It came from his dad's chewing tobacco—YUCK! A few minutes later, it happened again. I watched as his father leaned slightly towards the window and spit his tobacco juice approximately two feet out the window, where it immediately took a quick sharp left turn back towards my open window. As the tobacco juice flew back towards me I tried to take cover. Even though I attempted to duck out of the way, some of that brown juice found my forehead and the back of the seat. We both laughed spiritedly; I began to smell like chew tobacco. I'm not sure if his father ever knew why we were laughing. Maybe he did. I never asked him to quit spitting his chew. Kids just didn't say anything in those days to an adult. After that second incident, I decided to close the window three quarters of the way up and that basically did the trick. But I do remember I was grateful he didn't chew on the way home.

Lesson #28: Never sit behind the driver with the window down when the driver chews tobacco!

Occasionally I would ride with my father, who would usually smoke a cigarette in the car. Again I would be expected to sit in the back seat. The aroma from the smoke along with sitting in the back seat of the car would make me nauseous and light-headed. During the summer it was tolerable because I could put the window down, and the breeze would make me feel comfortable. But in the winter we were not permitted to open the rear car window. If we did without permission, look out! My father was a strict disciplinarian; he believed his way was the right and only way. I never argued with my father; no one in our family did. Dad was the boss.

During the winter the roads were never salted, and we never experienced clean roads after a snowfall. Families, including fathers, mothers, and children, would shovel out their driveways and make an effort to clear the road in front of their homes. Families who heated their homes with coal furnaces would lay ashes down to give traction to cars attempting to climb the inclined roads in our community. It worked just about every time.

Lesson #29: Think twice before wasting anything. Even coal ashes can be useful.

One winter day my father lit up a cigarette with the car heater on, and the smoke got so bad that I began to cough. I got brave and asked my father if he would please open the window. He obliged by opening his little side-vent of the front window, causing some air to circulate, but it was only small relief. It will come as no surprise when I point out that I wasn't anxious to ride in my father's car, particularly during the winter.

During the early fifties, the roads in High Park were "paved" with dirt. When a car rode by, the dirt would fly. The best thing we could do was just hold our breath and close our eyes. If we didn't, we would choke on the dust. Usually in late July a dump truck would drive through the neighborhood spreading red-dog gravel on the streets, filling in the potholes that developed during the winter and spring. Then another truck would scrape the roads level. This was our version of "road repair." Red-dog was a by-product of coal being used by the steel mills.

One thing we had that most neighbors didn't have was a garage. Our garage was made of concrete block and included two car spaces, a large workbench in the rear of the building, and a walk-up attic on the second floor. We never played inside the garage because it was "Dad's Place." He had his car, tools, and other equipment there. That is where my dad did all his oil changes and car repairs. He had a pulley chain that pulled the car up, so he could work safely under the vehicle. My dad sharpened knives, axes, and saws on his sander.

He took pleasure in helping us repair our bikes, sleds, and base-ball bats. Ladders, hoses, shovels, picks, hammers, and all of his other tools had their places in Dad's garage. He had every nail, screw, and washer that a household could ever need. Our garage was a man's world, and my dad was the "fix-it man." I truly believe that this place, the garage, was his therapy center.

Lesson #30: With a little teamwork and skilled persistence, big things can be accomplished.

Chapter 18

First Grade School: Passing Gas in Public and Other New Experiences

The High Park School, built around 1890, was a two-room red brick schoolhouse with six grades. The two rooms were sectioned off with three grades in one room and the other three grades in the second room.

Mrs. Campbell was my first and second grade teacher. She taught all three grades in that one room. I definitely remember my first day of school. My mother took me, and Mrs. Campbell placed me in the second seat of the first row. I sat down and looked back and saw my mother walking out the back door. I began to cry. I cried so hard that I didn't stop crying until my mother picked me up after school that day.

One of my memorable experiences in first grade occurred the last day before Christmas school vacation. It was snowing outside, and everyone was anticipating Christmas. All first graders were in the first row, about eight of us. Second graders were in the second row, third graders in the third and fourth rows. It was near the end of the school day, and everyone was excited. Mrs. Campbell permitted everyone to talk that day, but only in a low tone. All the students were talking at the same time about Christmas and excitedly telling each other what he or she wanted from Santa Claus.

All of a sudden I felt a major build-up of gas. I had never passed gas before in a public forum, at least never that I remember. The gas began to hurt my stomach. I felt pain and pressure. So I told myself just leave it out softly and no one would know. Then it happened. Without too much provocation and with little movement in my seat, a loud noise came from my backside. It was my first public gas pass. My fellow students around me began to laugh. They all knew it was me.

I was so embarrassed that I wanted to crawl under my seat. To this day I'm not sure if Mrs. Campbell heard that uncontrolled noise or just plain ignored it, but in a controlled voice she asked the students to keep the noise down if they wanted to continue talking. God bless her, she saved the day for me.

Lesson #31: Never trust the idea that flatulence can be controlled.

I remember a little girl named Patti from the spring of my first year in school. Her parents owned a farm and lived in the lower section of High Park. They also owned the green fields west of our community that were used to fatten the cows before the meat processing procedure. On certain days, when the winds blew west to east, the farm would send an unpleasant odor through the entire neighborhood. That's why High Park always had "cow flies."

I don't remember why or how it got started, but if anyone gave Patti candy or some gum, she would sneak up to the teacher's desk and snatch a pencil or crayon. At that age, I couldn't believe that this brave little girl would do a double dare, especially not one that involved sneaking past a teacher. Patti always played her trick when the teacher was three aisles away. We would look in awe and giggle quietly. These impressive feats would last only a few seconds, and she got away with it more than a few times. Eventually, though, Mrs. Campbell happened to glance over and catch her in the act.

Mrs. Campbell never said a word. At recess that day, little Patti stood quietly outside, near the school's water pump, with a cake of Ivory soap in her mouth. I'll bet she stood there for at least fifteen minutes. She never moved until it was time to go back into class. I can still see her standing there at the end of recess as our teacher took the soap out of her mouth, put her arm around Patti's shoulders, and talked quietly with her as they walked together into school. After we were seated, the teacher came over to the children sitting next to her and pointed her finger at us and warned us never to ask her to try any more shenanigans. As Mrs. Campbell spoke, all eyes were locked on her as we shook our heads in agreement. It never happened again.

Lesson #32: Girls can be just as brave as boys, but teachers don't like to see children talking each other into breaking rules.

Chapter 19

Second Grade: Love and School Chores

In second grade Mrs. Campbell was again my teacher. Not too many things changed, except there was a little girl in first grade who sat catty-corner to the left of me. I developed a crush on her. I will never forget her name: Linda. She was a blond beauty. She was pretty and friendly. What more could a guy my age ask for? The night before Valentine's Day, my mother gave me a packet of Valentine cards to give to my friends at school. I believe I had ten cards to give out. I signed every card and matched up the kids with the cards.

I picked out a special card for Linda. It was the most special Valentine's Day card I could find in the packet, and I signed it. The card said, "BE MY VALENTINE" (circled within a heart). On Valentine's Day afternoon, Mrs. Campbell permitted the students to walk around the room delivering cards to each other's desks. The room was filled with laughter, unorganized movement, and excited anticipation. In an orderly fashion, I gave my Valentine's Day cards out to my friends. Finally I walked over to Linda's desk.

I was sweating profusely. I presented her with my Valentine Card. I walked quickly to my desk, sat down, and waited.

When the teacher said we could open our Valentine cards, I watched Linda's every move. When she opened mine, she turned and smiled at me with that beautiful face and big blue eyes. I was in seventh heaven. It was a moment I have never forgotten. After that experience, I knew what love was all about. I felt bad for those kids who received only a few Valentine cards. It was one of the worst kinds of public humiliation a grade-schooler could experience. Today, my grandchildren inform me that every child in their classes both gives and receives Valentine cards.

Lesson #33: Love is always special, and first love is extra special.

School wasn't always cards and crushes. There were lots of rules too. If we wanted to get a drink of water, we had to get permission from the teacher to go to the back of the room near the coal furnace where a large, silver bucket of water and a ladle were located. The water came from the outside well equipped with a hand pump. The water was always cold no matter the time of year. I can't remember anyone ever getting sick from drinking the water or sharing the same ladle.

That large coal-fired furnace located in the back of the classroom heated the school well, as long as it was kept stoked. When additional coal was needed for the furnace, Mrs. Campbell would ask for a volunteer. We boys always wanted to be the one selected, so we were always quick to raise our hands with pleading in our voices. It was an honor to be chosen by the teacher to go to the coal shed approximately twenty-five yards from the school. We would carry the coal bucket to the outside coal shed, shovel the coal into the bucket, and then return as fast as we could. She would always thank us with a hug before returning us to our seats.

I recall the days when the weather was cold and we had to go to the bathroom. The school bathroom was adjacent to the coal shed. The bathroom was an "outhouse" which had separate entries for girls and boys. This was **not** a place where anyone wanted to linger. First, it had a distinct odor. Second, it was just as cold inside as it was outside. So the key was to do what needed to be done and return as quickly as possible to the warm schoolroom.

I have fond memories of attending school at High Park. Those days were fun and enjoyable. I wish today that I could thank Mrs. Campbell for being such a wonderful and genuine teacher. She had the patience of a saint. She was a perfect fit for the children of High Park.

Lesson #34: It often takes time to realize how grateful we can be for people who have made the biggest differences in our lives— people like teachers.

Chapter 20

Catholic School: Third Grade Adjustments

For whatever reason, my mother decided to transfer me to a Catholic school, Sacred Heart in Jeannette, for third grade. I'm assured that the main reason was because my brothers attended school there. My third grade teacher was Sister Gabriel; her disciplinary practices were much different from Mrs. Campbell's. If a student misbehaved or disrupted her class, she used physical punishment to restore discipline. I don't believe I was one of her favorite students. I never saw a nun before third grade, and when I saw her, I couldn't believe how she was dressed. The nuns were from the Benedictine order. They dressed in full habit: a black robe and a black veil with a white head cover around their faces. Our third grade class had approximately fifty students. Sacred Heart students were different. At the beginning they were not as friendly or sociable as the children at my old school.

High Park had only eight kids in the second grade. I truly missed the High Park School and its friendly atmosphere. And I missed the sight of Skippy, my dog, waiting for me after school to walk me home.

During my first few months attending Catholic school, I was lonely and confused. Every morning before the school day began, our teacher would check out our required dress code. The girls wore navy blue uniforms with white blouses, and the boys wore light brown khakis with a shirt. After the check was over, we left our schoolroom to attend Mass. We walked two by two, no talking, to our assigned pews. During Mass, we were forbidden to put our buttocks on the seat when kneeling. We had to kneel straight up. After Mass, we would walk in the same orderly fashion from church back to our classroom. If we talked, got out of line, or failed to follow her rules, Sister Gabriel would take matters into her own hands.

The first time a student in our class failed to follow the rules, I couldn't believe what happened. The kid behind me was talking and acting up, but Sister Gabriel wasn't amused. Back in our classroom, Sister Gabriel ordered the boy to come to the front. When he did, Sister Gabriel asked the boy to hold out one of his hands—palm up. She proceeded to "whack" him twice with an eighteen-inch ruler. The little boy walked back to his seat crying. I will never forget that experience. It was shocking to me!

Our first subject every day was Catechism. That usually lasted for forty-five minutes. It was all new to me: learning the Ten Commandments, the history of Jesus's life, and the crucifixion. I always believed the nuns at times embellished the Bible stories somewhat, but I couldn't prove it.

Something else was different in that school, and it wasn't so bad. We had indoor plumbing! Going to the bathroom indoors and drinking water out of a fountain was completely unique. And the school's heat came from a furnace in the basement. Unbelievable!

About eight weeks into the school year, I finally began to adjust. I began to enjoy school and the kids. Then one day I felt something hit me in the back of the head. I didn't know what it was until a few days later when the object, a small wad of wet paper, landed on my desk. I turned around to see who had thrown the "spit ball." The attacker went undetected that time.

Finally, later that week when I was hit by my daily "spit ball," I happened to turn around in time to see the culprit. I was furious and mad as you know what. This kid was using a straw to shoot the "spit ball" at me from ten feet away.

At lunchtime I met my foe in the school play yard, and a fight broke out between us. I knew how to take punishment, and I also knew how to dish it out. I had two older brothers who had taught me how to fight and defend myself.

The yard became a screaming arena of onlookers as I got the upper hand and won my first schoolyard fistfight. But the teacher on patrol that day happened to be our own Sister Gabriel. She grabbed the two of us by our collars and hauled us into the class-room. She shoved us into our seats and proceeded to call us "troublemakers." I carried that label for the rest of my days in third grade. I never understood why she didn't even ask us why we were fighting.

When all the kids returned from lunch/recess, she called the two of us to the front of the room and told us to put out one of our hands, palm up. I went first, but not by choice. She then smacked the palm of my hand three times. It stung! Tears welled up in my eyes, but I didn't cry. She gave the same punishment to my opponent; same results. I didn't realize it at that time, but this incident changed my fellow schoolmates' perspective of me. From then on, I became one of "the tough kids" in third grade because I whipped a kid who was considered one of the toughest guys in the class. By the way, that kid never threw another spitball at me again.

Lesson #35: It's easier to get a bad reputation than it is to get rid of one.

Fighting was rare but not uncommon on the school play yard because someone always wanted to test his strength against someone else. When I had to fight, I would meet the kid off school property in an alley. I never picked a fight, but trouble sometimes found me during the next five years.

I never told my mother about these fighting incidents because I was afraid that I would be punished at home too. I would rather meet the fate of my opponent than the fate of my father.

Lesson #36: Trouble sometimes finds us, and we must be prepared to defend ourselves.

I met Don and Ron Watkoski, identical twins, in third grade right after my scuffle. They were in my class next to the window about five rows across from me. They were among the first kids to talk to me after school that day. They congratulated me along with other kids who said that the other boy deserved what he got from me. I made many new friends that week. I found out that day that Don and Ron lived in High Park on the other side of Baughman Avenue. This was approximately five blocks from where I lived, but they never went to the High Park School.

We developed a fast friendship that has lasted to this day. Before I met Don and Ron, one of my brothers was usually responsible for walking me to and from school. From the following day forward, I didn't need my brothers to walk me home anymore. I began walking to and from school with the twins every day. The round trip was almost a three-mile journey. We walked the next five and a half years together.

Rain, snow, or shine—cold or hot—we walked every day. Believe it or not, we never had a cancellation of school because of snow. It wasn't hard walking to school, but going home was the challenge. Part of the journey was walking up a very steep grade, approximately a half-mile uphill before reaching High Park. The first part of the steep grade was a dirt road, while the last half meandered on a path between trees and bushes. During those walks to and from school, we would talk about everything, including school, sports, and girls.

Lesson #37: We can often find a place for ourselves, even in completely new situations.

One Christmas while I was attending Mass at the Ascension Catholic Church in Jeannette, the priest spoke from the pulpit and asked the young children in attendance if anyone would be interested in becoming an altar boy. I liked the idea, so I decided to sign up and go for it. It took me three months to learn the Latin prayers and the procedures for serving as an altar boy. Finally I got the call from Father James one day to serve the 6:30 a.m. Sunday Mass. I did remember all my Latin prayers that day, but

I needed Father's assistance with the serving part of the washing of the hands and serving of the wine. I was so nervous. After that first experience, Father James asked me if I could serve the 8:00 a.m., Monday through Friday Mass the following week. I told him I would have to check with Sister Gabriel, my third-grade teacher. He told me to let him know if I needed any help getting permission.

I went to school Monday morning and approached Sister Gabriel with my request to be excused until 9:00 a.m. every day the following week so I could serve daily Mass at Ascension Church. I remember the peculiar look on her face: she was in shock. She looked at me and said, "Of course," with a sheepish grin. From that moment on and for the rest of the year, she treated me with more respect and showed a little more kindness to me. I made it through the third grade, and I truly enjoyed being an altar boy during my adolescent years. It was a great experience and occasionally got me out of Catechism class.

Lesson #38: Playing politics can be good for the soul.

Chapter 21

Respect, Honor, Justice, and Obedience

Fourth and fifth grades were fun times for me. I had adjusted to school, had friends, and Sister Mary and Mrs. Hart were nothing but great teachers. We continued to have forty to fifty students in our class, but school was enjoyable. We began to realize girls were "made to be teased." During these years, my mother didn't have to remind me to brush my teeth or comb my hair before leaving for school. Life was good to me in those days. I continued to find out more about who I was.

I also found out that there really was no such thing as a free lunch. Literally, if we forgot to bring a lunch to school, we didn't eat until we got home. I believe I forgot my lunch only once in the six years I attended Sacred Heart School. Once in a while our parents would give us milk money, fifteen cents a week or three cents per day. The milk in school was usually warm by lunchtime, so I always saved my milk money and spent it on "penny" candy or a five-cent candy bar. Penny candy was really penny candy. Some of my favorites were Bit O'Honey, Root Beer Barrels, Tootsie Roll Midgets, Wax Bottles with liquid, and Candy Cigarettes; and they were just a few of the penny candies I enjoyed when I had only a few cents in my pocket. I got more satisfaction from eating candy than I did from drinking warm milk.

My friends and I always shared our candy or pop (soda) with each other. Anyone who didn't would have to find new friends before long. Oh yes, sometimes a disagreement would ensue because someone took too much of the candy bar being shared. Our name for a person that greedy was "HOG."

Sharing was a way of life in our early fifties world. It was a necessary part of growing up and being a partner to our friends. The Ten Commandments, good judgment, and common sense governed our lives.

We were taught to know the difference between right and wrong and to stand up and take responsibility for our actions.

> **Lesson #39:** These formative years taught me respect, honor, justice, and obedience. It was these lessons learned at home, at school, and with my friends that made me who and what I am today.

Chapter 22

Riding Bikes

I had been watching my brother Ron ride his Schwinn bike for years, and oh how I wanted to ride his bike! Some days I would watch him coming home, staring with amazement as he rode down Pine Street; his body appeared motionless as if he were gliding in the wind. One summer day when my brother was not around, I decided to ride his bike even though I knew I should have asked for his permission first. It looked so easy although I had never ridden a two wheel bike before. I figured it couldn't be *that* difficult.

Well, I pushed the bike from the garage area to the top of our gravel driveway. I took a deep breath and proceeded to put my left foot on the upper pedal while pushing with the same foot; I jumped onto the seat with my backside: success. I began awkwardly steering the bike forward. As I reached for the bottom pedal with my right foot, I realized that my right leg wasn't long enough to reach the pedal. I panicked! I turned the handlebars left then right, lost control and crashed the bike on the dirt road. Except for a few minor dents on the bike and my bruised ego, I was OK. That's when I realized that my big brother's bike seat was too high for me to ride. That was a major problem.

When my brother came home that evening, I confessed to him about my misadventure. I provided him with the ugly details of my effort. He laughed and thought it was funny, but at the same time he warned me that I should ask him for approval if I ever wanted to ride it again. About a week later, I approached my brother Ron to see if he was interested in selling his bike to me. After a few minutes of negotiations, we agreed to a bill of sale for ten dollars and one free bike-riding lesson.

He wanted the money within two weeks or the deal was off. I immediately raced up to the secret hiding place in my room to see how much money I had saved from caddying. I had exactly $5.25. But within a week I saved enough money from caddying that I was able to present my brother with the agreed amount. He was pleasantly surprised and lived up to his part of the agreement. He adjusted the bike seat and showed me how to stand on the pedals while pedaling the bike.

Within a couple of days I was riding "my bike" as though I had been riding all summer. Finally my parents permitted me to ride by myself to the playground. That evening after dinner I struggled riding my bike up Pine Street because of the slight upward grade. I finally made it to the crest of the road with most of my energy used up, but, although tired, I had a big smile on my face. I rode onto the playground and began showing my friends my slightly used, "new" bike. Most of my friends didn't have bicycles.

Lesson #40: Working hard and saving money for special purchases can be very satisfying.

Later that week, Jay came over to my house and wanted to try riding my bike. But there was one serious concern: Jay couldn't ride a two-wheeler. Over the course of the next week, I taught my friend how to ride.

Just a few weeks later, Jay called me on the telephone with excitement in his voice. He asked me to come over to his house as soon as possible. Within minutes I stood at his back porch and called for him. He came to the door and asked me, with a smile on his face, to walk around to the front of the house. There, to my surprise, was Jay's brand new, red Schwinn bike—a gift from his parents. Not only was it a "new-new" bike, but it also had brake handles and gear shifts on the handle bars. That was high-tech in the early fifties. By this time, our friend Perry had arrived and was carefully looking over Jay's bike. Both of us were in awe. After touching the metal, the tires, and the brakes on the handlebars, Jay decided to take a ride. Since he already knew how to ride by practicing on my bicycle, he effortlessly jumped on his new bike and began to pedal down the hill with speed and balance. It didn't take long at all for him to race to the bottom of Cort Street, round the corner to the right with ease, and head up First Street, moving swiftly out of sight.

We all knew where he was going, and a few minutes later we watched him come down Pine Street turning right onto Cort Street at an amazing pace. His lap ended with a precision stop in front of us—easy as could be! We were in disbelief. It was faster than any bike we'd ever seen, especially ours. Our bikes, Perry's and mine, were "vintage" quality. Our "classics" couldn't compete with his speed machine. After much prodding and begging, Jay agreed to let me take his bike for a ride.

I will never forget that bike ride for as long as I live. Before I got on the bike, Jay explained the braking system. But my mind was not focused on the braking system. I was ready to fly! I put my hands on the handlebars, pushed the pedal forward, and the bike began moving swiftly down Cort Street. While moving, I adjusted the gears, attempting to get the maximum speed from the bike. As I approached the end of Cort Street, I applied the minimum brake necessary to make the turn and begin racing up First Street. I turned right at the next corner and shifted gears to make my way up the hill on Cyprus Street. I was so nervous that I believe I used the wrong gear going up the street and had to get off and push the bike up the steepest part of the hill. I ran up the hill, rolling the bike beside me, until I reached Pine Street. Then I jumped back on the bike and began pedaling again. I was imagining myself as a race car driver. My speed increased every few yards as I rode down the hill, turning right onto Cort Street with only a minimum amount of braking. I was back to full speed over the last fifty yards of the route back to Jay's house. As I got closer to Jay and Perry, I applied *only* the left brake at full force as I had earlier. I did not know that the left brake handle only worked the front brake and not the rear brake, so I was in big trouble. The front brakes locked, and the back of the bike acted accordingly. My body "gently" flew over the handlebars with the back end of the bike following me. I landed softly on the dirt road with the bike still in hand.

I immediately heard Jay screaming at me for wrecking his bike. He didn't ask if I was hurt. I don't think he cared at that moment about me. I proceeded to lift myself up off the road and noticed blood on my hands and arms while Jay picked up the bike and began to inspect it for damage. He asked me why I hadn't applied both brakes on the bike. I explained I was left-handed and thought that the left brake applied to both the front and back. I apologized profusely while attempting to explain to him that I wasn't aware that the right side had brakes too. Damage to the bike was minimal—just a few scratches on the bike and seat. But Jay was upset. Needless to say, Perry did *not* get to ride Jay's bike that day.

It was weeks before Jay forgave me, but I did ride his bike again, and of course he rode mine while we got back to enjoying our friendship.

Lesson #41: It's always a good idea to pay attention whenever someone is explaining how things work.

Chapter 23

Movies

During the fifties, movies were produced, formatted, and fashioned for children of all ages—including teenagers and adults. Other than cartoons, movies were focused on cowboy heroes, war stories of love and honor, gangster movies directed at crime and justice and, to lighten the day, slapstick comedy. With very few people having television, movie theaters gave us all a place to find peace and entertainment.

My first experience going to the movies was rather frightening. I was only five years old, and my mother encouraged my eight-year-old brother Rich to take me. Up to that point, I had never watched television and had never been in a movie theater. We went to see *The Wizard of Oz*.

The first thing I noticed when we walked into the theater was the aroma of popcorn. Secondly I was overwhelmed by the sight of the colorful brightly lit candy case filled with an amazing assortment of candies. My brother and I had no additional money to spend on any of those treats. As I was enjoying the sights and smells, my brother took me by the hand and led me through a door to a dark room inside the theater and to our seats, where we waited for the movie to begin. I really didn't know what to expect. As the first light appeared on the screen, I quickly noticed I couldn't see the full screen because of the person sitting in front of me. I had to sit on my legs, so I could see. Within minutes I was watching the World News, then a cartoon, and then— *finally*—the movie began. The large screen fascinated me. The movie started out in black and white and later switched to color. Suddenly the tornado scene startled me; I tried to curl up closer to my brother, but he pushed me away. I was all alone watching the movie in a dark, scary place.

I began crying quietly, and then I got really upset when the Wicked Witch of the West sent the flying monkeys after Dorothy. That was it for me. I couldn't stand it. I started sobbing loudly and begged my brother to take me home. All of sudden, Rich roughly grabbed my hand and led me to the back of the theater. He had no intention of taking me home, so he asked the manager permission to call home. I heard him talking to my mother, explaining the situation to her. Finally he hung up the phone. He looked at me and said, "Dad's coming to get you." I stood alone inside the entrance area near the candy case, again smelling the popcorn. I stopped crying out loud, but I was still whimpering a little. My brother stood inside the door of the theater so he could watch the movie and still keep an eye on his five-year-old brother.

At that time, we lived in Jeanette near the Ascension Church on Division Street, just a few blocks from the Manos Theater. It wasn't very long until my dad arrived. I was sniffling a little when

I told him about the scary movie. He never said a word. He just took my hand, and we walked home together; I felt safe again. My dad was a man of few words, but I knew by the look in his eyes that he understood.

Yes, I did go back to the movies, but it wasn't until we moved to High Park. I was a little older, and again I went with my brother Rich. My cousin Tommy went along and brought his brother Jerry. Tommy was the same age as my brother, and Jerry was a tad younger than I. On that eventful Saturday afternoon, we watched at least twenty-five cartoons and the upcoming features. The total show lasted approximately ninety minutes. I would go to these Saturday matinees a couple of times a year during my early child-hood years.

The Saturday matinees were always packed with screaming kids, and the noise level was deafening. It was hard to hear what the cartoon characters were saying. The highlight for the kids, including me, was to throw candy at each other. Can you believe it? I always made sure I ate my candy, and then by crawling on the theater floor I would look for pieces of candy to throw at the others. There was no way I was going to waste my candy that way! We would throw the candy at kids in front of us, and when they turned around and looked at us, we would point over in another direction claiming those kids threw the candy. We thought this was great fun.

As I got older, there would always be a group of friends going to the movies. My mother would give me twenty-five cents to spend. First we would go to the ice cream parlor next to the theater, where we bought ourselves a Klondike Bar (a chocolate covered vanilla ice cream bar). We weren't allowed to bring any food or drink into the theater. So we would hide the ice cream bars in our coat pockets and sneak them into the theater. Sometimes we would have to wait in line fifteen to twenty minutes before entering the theater, and our ice cream bars by that time were melting in our pockets. We didn't care. We ate them anyway.

The movie cost fourteen cents, and the Klondike Bar was ten cents. After the movie we would go to the candy store and buy a penny piece of candy to eat on the way home.

In the spring of my first year (third grade) attending Sacred Heart Catholic School, the entire school went to see *The Robe*. This was a movie depicting the crucifixion of Jesus Christ. The timing for taking us to this movie was perfect. It was during Lent, and the Crucifixion was the "hot topic" of our classroom discussion. I noticed as a young student, from my vantage point, that this movie had a profound effect on us because of our belief. The nuns wanted this effect on their students and hoped to make us all better Catholics. I'm sure that, for many of the students, it did have that effect.

Lesson #42: It's best to always appreciate everyone's good intentions.

Movies were never a major part of my childhood. One of the main reasons was financial; my parents didn't have money to send us to the movies all the time. But when we did go, it was a special event because the movies I went to see involved a scary monster, a bloody war, or a shoot-it-out cowboy adventure. John Wayne was every child's hero, including mine. We would talk for weeks about any movie we had seen, and on occasion we would play out a cowboy or military part with guns and imitate scary monsters.

On one occasion, Jay and I went to see a scary monster movie. I believe it was *Abbott and Costello Meet Frankenstein*. A few days later we were sitting on our front porch after dark with my oldest brother Ron. We were talking about the scary monster movie we had just seen and began asking my brother pointed questions about monsters. "Are monsters really real?" Ron was five years older than we, so we figured he was an expert on this issue.

This was a dumb question to ask an older brother who, at any time, would have liked to put the fear of God in us. Ron, with an honest face, told us that there were monsters lurking everywhere, particularly in the woods at night. He even shared a secret with us. He declared that just a few nights before, he thought he saw the green eyes of a monster in the nearby stretch of woods between Jay's house and ours. After hearing movement in the woods, frightened, he ran home as fast as his legs could carry him. Then with a soft voice he claimed that the monster may be living in the upper part of the woods near the road or hiding in the bushes nearby. In the same tone of voice, we asked him what it looked like. My brother said he believed, from what he could see, it had a hairy face and green eyes. He said it could even be a werewolf, but he wasn't sure.

We all knew that Jay had a serious problem: he had to walk home through that small, narrow, wooded area, and it was late—after 9:00 p.m. There were no streetlights. After this intense discussion, Ron claimed he was tired and was going to bed.

Because Jay was scared and we both believed in monsters, he decided not to take the usual shortcut—walking directly through our yard, then through a neighbor's yard to a thin line of trees and bushes and crossing an alley to his house, a route of approximately one hundred yards. He believed his other choice was safer: through our tree-lined yard to Pine Street, walking up the street to an alley, and then turning left down the alley to his house. This route was more than twice the length of our usual *"monster-laden"* shortcut.

You must keep in mind that during this era there were no streetlights and few neighbors. And neighbors rarely turned on their porch lights unless someone came knocking at their doors. A dark night could be very, very dark (and scary) for young boys with overactive imaginations.

Before starting his journey home, he asked me to turn on our porch light and walk with him. I said, "Jay, are you crazy?" I was scared too and said, "No way." He then pleaded with me to stand on the front porch and talk to him until he made his way home. I agreed to that request. I turned on the porch light, stood on the front porch, and watched Jay begin his journey home. As he barely made it to the end of our property line, which was lined with pine trees that stretched across our front yard, he suddenly came running back to the house. Breathing heavily and very excited, Jay claimed he heard something moving in the pine trees. I started to laugh and called him a "scaredy-cat." Then I double dared him to walk home. At that point, he wanted no part of any double dare. He pleaded with me to walk him beyond our row of pine trees to the top of the road. Although with much anxiety, I worked up my courage and consented.

Jay led the way through the pine trees. Suddenly my brother Ron jumped out of hiding and let out a big roar, frightening Jay and me almost to death. We both screamed simultaneously as Ron began to laugh. Jay started crying, and I couldn't talk or run. Ron got the biggest thrill out of scaring us that evening. After this shocking experience, Jay begged my brother to walk him home. Finally, after more prodding, Ron did walk Jay home, but he never let us forget this scary incident.

Lesson #43: Never ask older brothers about scary monsters.

Chapter 24

Parents

In that era of stay-at-home moms, a mother's uniform for a normal day included a dress with an apron wrapped around her waist. Whether it was ninety degrees or ten degrees outside, the dress code rarely changed.

Things were quite consistent on Mondays for mothers. This was Laundry Day. We could count on it. The wringer washer, washboard, clothespins, rope lines connected to metal/wood posts, clothesline props, and metal stretchers were all key components of laundry day. Laundry was a time-consuming venture for moms during this time period. It usually took most of the daylight hours to do the washing and drying of the clothes outside. There were no automatic washers or clothes dryers. Mothers would get up early in the morning to wash their clothes and by mid-morning have the wash hung outside drying on the clothesline.

Leg stretchers were placed into the legs of jeans and pants so they would have a sharp crease and wouldn't get wrinkled. Creases were cool on jeans at that time. Hopefully by mid-afternoon the clothes would be dry and would be taken down by hand off the line, folded and put into a clothesbasket, and carried back to the house. Then they were taken into the house to be placed in drawers and closets. Occasionally my friends and I would tease each other about our mothers' undergarments that were hanging on the clothesline.

Thursdays and Sundays were my mother's pasta dinner days. Thursday was rigatoni with red meat sauce. Sunday was standard capellini with red meat sauce and fried chicken with our spaghetti.

What was unique about our family dinners was that my mother always placed one large salad bowl on the table. There were no individual salad bowls for the Gaudi family! This huge salad bowl was strategically placed in the center of our dining room table, where all members of our family could reach it with ease. We all used our dinner forks for our salads. Depending on the season, Mom's salad usually included lettuce, tomatoes, carrots, onions, celery, cucumbers, and peppers. Mom's special salad dressing never changed: vinegar and oil with her secret seasonings. Oh, by the way, if any of our friends showed up for dinner, they too participated in the salad-sharing ritual.

Mom later in life attempted to explain to me how the dressing was made, but I never could duplicate the taste. She never used a recipe.

We always had bread and dessert with our meals. My mother made the *best* homemade bread and baked goods. As far as our family was concerned, she was the best cook in the neighborhood, maybe the world. All my friends loved her homemade bread and desserts, including cookies, cakes, and pies. She always welcomed any of our friends to join us if they showed up at dinnertime.

During the school year, Mom always prepared lunch for the entire family—my dad, her three sons, and daughter Judy, who came along much later. Our school lunch, always placed in a brown paper bag, consisted of sandwiches, fruit(s), and a dessert (usually cookies, cake, or sometimes a candy bar). Fruit was placed at the bottom of the brown bag, followed by the sandwiches, and the dessert was always on top. Our school sandwiches were wrapped in wax paper. We were always reminded to bring the brown paper bag home for re-use. My dad's lunch included the same menu as ours, but he carried his in a black metal lunch bucket. The only thing different about his lunch was that it featured a thermos, always filled with coffee.

I can remember my mom cutting steak and chopping vegetables at the kitchen sink with the same cutting board and with the same knife. It's amazing that we never got food poisoning. My mom used to defrost hamburger and chicken on the same counter.

Mothers during that era did a lot of canning. Canning of vegetables (mainly tomatoes), and fruits (pears and peaches) was a major chore or project for High Park's mothers. Moms also made jellies and jams—cherry, peach, elderberry, and grape. This provided us with a variety of jellies and jams to eat any time of the year. They also canned peppers that were great with sandwiches. Families stored their canned goods on shelves in the basement, keeping them cool in all seasons. This stockpiling enabled families to eat more nutritiously and economically.

During the week my mother dealt with a variety of efficient small-business people. The "Egg Lady" came on Thursday to deliver eggs in her old 1942 Studebaker. On Mondays and Fridays the "Milkman," who was a dairy farmer, brought our milk in an old delivery truck. The cream at times popped the paper cap on the glass bottles. The "Bread Man" came every other Friday, bringing fresh loaves of bread to our house as needed. Finally, I remember the insurance man would come to the house every so often, I believe quarterly, and Mom would pay him for Dad's life insurance policy. All of these transactions were done in cash.

Holidays and summer family reunions were always held at my parents' house. My parents always made everyone feel welcome; my mom was a great hostess. Living at the end of Pine Street, we had a big yard with numerous shade trees, and adults could sit back, relax, and enjoy themselves while the kids played safely.

Lesson #44: There is no hospitality like Mom's hospitality and no cooking better than Mom's.

Chapter 25

Christmas

Christmas Eve was a special time for our traditional family meal of Bagna Caoda. Bagna Caoda in Italian means "hot dip." In addition to Bagna Caoda, these eventful meals included other classic fish dishes like smelts and baccala. The Bagna Caoda is still a tradition in my household today.

Bagna Caoda
6 cloves of garlic, minced

2 sticks of butter

1/3 cup of oil

2 cans of flat anchovies

First, add the butter at a low heat. Continue to stir until the butter melts; don't burn the butter. Stir constantly, then add the oil and continue to stir. When it begins to boil, turn the temperature down. Next, add the garlic; stir every ten seconds until the garlic gets soft (approximately ten minutes). Add the anchovies; continue to stir. Within a few minutes, the Bagna Caoda is ready to serve. Total preparation time is about twenty to twenty-five minutes. The key to making Bagna Caoda is continuous stirring over low heat so the butter doesn't burn.

Eating Bagna Caoda: Use any vegetable(s) desired (head lettuce, peppers, broccoli, celery, etc.). Dip vegetables into the Bagna Caoda using Italian bread to catch the drips. Eat the vegetable and then the bread laden with the Bagna Caoda drippings. Enjoy!

After Christmas Eve dinner, my family would all get together to play our instruments and sing our favorite Christmas carols. My dad played his harmonica, joining my brother Rich, who played the accordion. Ron, my oldest brother, who carried a handsome voice, would sing and the rest of the family would join in. Sometimes my mother and I would dance with my sister. The entire family would enjoy this special family moment. Later in life I joined the family ensemble by playing the guitar.

> **Lesson #45:** There is no place like home
> for the holidays—especially a home full of
> extended family and friends.

Christmas gifts were not as plentiful or fancy (or expensive) as they are today, but we did appreciate everything we received. We were always grateful for the gifts we received from our parents during the Christmas holiday. We knew that our parents were limited in what they could give us.

Relatives would never think of bringing a gift for the kids. It simply wasn't a practice in our family. When relatives came for a visit, my mother would provide a buffet meal fit for a king. The food usually included a baked turkey and ham, salami, capicola, cheeses, vegetables, candies, and a variety of Italian cookies for dessert. Refreshments for adults included wines, beer, and a variety of whiskeys. Kids drank water, milk, or Kool-Aid; rarely did we have "pop" or soda to drink.

As I stated before, we didn't have much, but my parents provided a wonderful display of food during the Christmas holiday. I always wonder if some of our relatives came to visit us only because of the food. Some families came empty handed, never bringing a gift for my mother or a bottle of wine for my dad. My parents never complained about it or cared. They were always happy to see visitors. Our house was always open to relatives and friends. It was truly a great time of the year for socializing and eating.

Lesson #46: My mother always made me and anyone else who came to our home feel wanted. People might forget what we do, but people don't forget how we made them feel.

One Christmas Eve, my father told our family a true story about the Christmas he and his family experienced when he was about nine years old. His father died earlier that year, and during the early 1930s era, in addition to the hardships of the Depression, the federal or state governments didn't have many handouts for families in distress. My father's family included eleven children, all living at home, and a mother who only spoke Italian. During this period of time, the Great Depression, there weren't many job opportunities for anyone. On their first Christmas morning after his father's death, his mother lined up all of the children according to their age in the living room. My dad said they were all excited, talking noisily. After all, it *was* Christmas morning. They weren't sure what gifts they were going to receive. He distinctly recalls his mother appearing before them with a large brown shopping bag. His mom started with the youngest; my dad was second in line, and she gave each child an orange and a hug for their Christmas present. That was the *only* Christmas present they received that year. Although disappointed, they all understood. My dad said his mom loved her children unconditionally. *He sensed it.*

Lesson #47: Always be grateful for what you receive.

Chapter 26

Death, Family, and Sharing

It was late spring of fifth grade when my dad's mother died. I had never experienced a family death until then. I can remember my mom and dad in the living room one evening, talking, a day after the passing of my grandmother. I heard my mother in a very soft tone comforting my dad, telling him that his mother led a good life and did a great job raising her children. Then I heard my father crying. This shocked me because I had never heard or seen my father cry. I will never ever forget that moment. I was saddened because of the hurt my father carried in his heart. My mother comforted my father as she held him in her arms. I had never seen that kind of interaction between my parents before that day.

The next day my father asked me to serve as the altar boy for his mother's funeral. Of course I agreed to do it, but I told my dad that I would need permission from the priest. Guess what? I had never served a funeral before. This would be my first as an altar boy. The service is still very clear in my mind. That may be due, in part, to the unique point of view I had from the altar. I watched everyone very closely as I performed my duties. It was very different from being in a pew.

During the service I thought all my relatives were staring at me. Afterward, they continued to stare at me as the priest and I moved around my grandmother's casket with the incense. It was somewhat unnerving. Thank God, Father James was presiding at the Mass. He was very calm and gentle. He provided all the necessary assistance to get me through that day. Everything went as well as could be expected for my dad and his family. All eleven siblings and their families were in attendance. I know my dad was very proud of me that day, not because he told me so, but because I saw it in his eyes.

As I look back on those days, it occurs to me that most affirmation was unspoken. I can't remember anyone ever telling my mom and dad what a great job they were doing raising their children. Parenting was more instinct. I truly believe my dad only knew what he experienced as a child and wanted his sons to grow up to become good American citizens. As far as I know, not a single person in High Park had ever been told that he was from a dysfunctional family.

My dad had only a seventh grade education because of his father's death. He had to drop out of school to help support the family. My mom had to quit school in the eleventh grade because my mother's parents separated. During that period in America, times were difficult because families didn't have the benefit of a safety net of government assistance.

Vacations during this period were only for the wealthy, not for factory workers. A vacation for a High Park family meant going to the mountains or state park for a day or visiting a relative for the weekend. Money was used for more practical things such as fixing a roof, buying a piece of furniture or a new washing machine, or repairing a car. And as for us kids, we didn't know any better. We lived in our own little world. As these pages show, we played and had fun without any real cares in the world.

Other things I remember from that period of my life:

- ✧ We didn't have bottled water. We drank— safely—from the outside spigot.
- ✧ We shared our soft drinks, which we called "pop," with our friends.
- ✧ A Popsicle had two pieces, and we always shared with a friend.
- ✧ We always shared our treats, an unwritten and absolute law.
- ✧ In the summertime, we would leave home in the morning and play all day.
- ✧ Parents didn't have to worry about not knowing exactly where we were.
- ✧ No matter where we were, we all knew to be home by dinnertime.
- ✧ And parents always sided with the teacher!

I have the utmost respect for my parents because of the challenges they encountered and overcame while doing without any federal, state, or local assistance. Families did struggle during this period when fathers were laid off from factory work or other jobs, but everyone managed to survive.

I can't ever remember my parents complaining about this country. My dad said one day, "When one door closes, another will open." There were Christmases when we received very few gifts, but my brothers, sister, and I understood. When Dad was not working at the plant, he did find odd jobs that kept our family fed and clothed and sheltered and out of debt. As a family, we survived as all families did.

My father and mother taught me a work ethic, respect for authority, the value of keeping promises, commitment to my faith, and the privilege of getting an education.

I guess the best way to end this chapter about my parents is to point out that we were, in our own way, like the Barone family on the sitcom, *Everybody Loves Raymond.* We didn't hug or kiss, but we knew we were a unit. The eyes and actions revealed the love and kindness my parents had for their children. Based on my past experience, I see many ways that parents and grandparents are different than they were in the 1950s. I love to hug my grandchildren and tell them I love them. I enjoy taking the grandkids to the movies, riding bikes, taking walks through the woods, and playing ball. They are at the center of attention in our household when they visit. During the fifties era, the grandparents were more interested in their own children, my parents; we grandkids would sit in the corner and listen or play outside.

> "Passing on a legacy—each of us leaves a thumbprint on the world, a record that we were here and who we were and what we did; your only choice is what kind of thumbprint you leave."
>
> — Sidney B. Simon

Lesson #48: A family legacy cannot be bought or sold. It can only be given as a free gift of sacrificial love from generation to generation.

Chapter 27

Friends

I am so blessed to have lived as long as I have. I wish to express my gratitude to those who helped me make it through those tough years: my parents, teachers, brothers, and my friends—especially my friends. Friends can alter a person's life; mine certainly have—for the better. Friends are and have been very important to me in my lifetime. My true friends are persons who like me for whom and what I am. Unconditional love and acceptance are the greatest gifts that friends can give.

As I reflect on my life from my current vantage point, I realize that some of my friends and family have died before having the chance to experience and appreciate this stage in life. My brother Ron, stepson Matthew, and my friends Carmen Ortuglio and Denny Parsons have all departed. I miss them all very much.

As we get older, it is easier to be positive. We care less about what other people think. I don't question myself anymore. I can't please everyone, so I don't try. I found out early in life that certain people, because of their opinions about the way a person thinks, looks, speaks, dresses will never want to be my friend. What a loss for them.

My memories of growing up in the fifties have a common theme. I found the greatest joys in the little things, like getting a nickel to buy a candy bar, or riding a bike with a friend on the handle bars, or just laughing at a friend who attempts to jump over a small creek, only to slip and fall into the water.

All of my experiences developed my character and helped me become the man I am today. Yes, there were times of sorrow and grief, but as I look back on those times, I smile. We never missed a beat; we had all of the "sweet freedoms" life had to offer. We didn't have all the extras that kids have today, but our happiness came from within—within our own imaginations, our own families, our own community.

My best friends during this era, Jay, Perry, and the twins Donnie and Ronnie, are still alive today. When we do see each other, sometimes years between visits, the time is filled with stories of joy and friendship and, yes, sometimes with tears.

Love to all who shared the fifties era in America. And to all who didn't, I'm sorry for what you missed; I wouldn't trade it for anything.

> "A true friend is someone who reaches for your hand and touches your heart. What lies behind us and what lies before us are tiny matters compared to what lies within us."
> —Ralph Waldo Emerson

"Many people will walk in and out of your life. But only true friends will leave footprints in your heart."

—Eleanor Roosevelt

Chapter 28
One Final Life Lesson Story

Before I end my book of childhood memories, I would like to leave a message that illustrates the qualities my friends and I learned growing up in the early fifties in High Park. It's best seen in a story my mom likes for me to tell about my High Park friends and my Down Syndrome cousin Pepe, who died recently. My mother's sister visited us with her family one summer day. My friends, my brothers, and I were playing a pickup baseball game on our field. I happened to see my uncle and his son Pepe walking near the playing field and watching us.

During a change of innings, I explained to the kids Pepe's condition and thought it would be nice if we invited him to play ball. When they all agreed, I asked my uncle if he would let Pepe play ball with us. At first my uncle was hesitant, but he finally gave in to the encouragement from the other kids and me. Pepe was two years younger than I, and I don't believe he had ever played baseball or even held a bat in his hands before because of his physical and mental condition. My friends understood Pepe's limitations and proceeded to take the appropriate action without any encouragement or directions.

When Pepe walked hesitantly over to the kids, they all smiled and welcomed him with reassuring handshakes and pats on the back. He smiled and immediately became more comfortable. We put Pepe at second base with a glove. He actually stood on second base. We all called his name out with excitement, which appeared to please him. His father watched with a small grin and clapped with enthusiasm. All the kids witnessed the father's joy. We also saw the happiness this brought to Pepe. No one dared to hit a ball to him, but we still made him feel part of the team. After the third out, our team came to bat.

Our team's first three batters all hit singles, and at that point we decided to give the bat to Pepe. Fate was in our hands, and we didn't know it. First of all, to have three consecutive singles hit during a pickup game is almost unheard of because of player errors, players stretching a single into an extra base hit, or the usual pop-ups and ground-outs. Pepe, having never played ball before, didn't know how to hold the bat. I patiently showed him how to hold it properly before he got into the batter's box.

Before Pepe stepped up to the plate, the pitcher moved in approximately halfway to home. The pitcher lobbed the first pitch softly so Pepe could at least attempt to make contact. The first pitch came, and it appeared that Pepe didn't know what to do. I could see Pepe was confused, so I helped him hold the bat. The pitcher again tossed the ball softly towards home plate. Pepe, with my assistance, swung at the next ball and hit a slow ground ball towards third base. The third baseman picked up the soft grounder and could have easily made a double play, but he willingly threw the ball over the second baseman's head into right field. Everyone from both teams started yelling, "Pepe, run to first! Run to first!"

Pepe, with my assistance, ran to first base slowly. But as he got to first base, everyone started to yell, "Run to second, run to second!" Awkwardly Pepe, with my assistance, ran towards second; he struggled to make it to the base. By the time Pepe got to second base, the right fielder had the ball. He understood everyone's intentions, so he intentionally threw the ball awkwardly to first base. Continuing our encouragement, we cheered as Pepe, with my assistance, ran toward third base. Everyone on the field and around the field was screaming, "Keep going, Pepe. Go!" As Pepe reached third base, I noticed his father getting caught up in the moment; he was yelling at Pepe, "Keep going!" As we rounded third, everyone was screaming, "Pepe, run home; run home!" I pointed him in the right direction, and Pepe, with little assistance, knew where to go and ran to home plate. As he touched home, all of the kids, including his father, gathered around Pepe and cheered him as a hero who had just hit a grand slam home run.

As his father approached us with tears of joy in his eyes, he said, "Thank you. I love all of you for what you did today for my son." As my uncle and Pepe walked slowly down Pine Street, holding each other's hands, we realized what a special moment we had just experienced. My Uncle Guy never forgot that day, and every time we were together after that, he would always give me a special smile. Later in life, when I was much older, he told me he never forgot the kindness and thoughtfulness displayed by those "High Park Kids."

Lesson #49: One brief moment of spontaneous kindness can become a lifetime treasure.

Since I have moved away from Jeannette, I don't see Perry or his younger brother Mike very often—both enjoy hunting and fishing. They have remained my friends throughout my life. Seldom do I see the twins, Donnie and Ronnie, but it is always with a smile of friendship and shared memories. Both are retired and doing the things they like to do: hunting and fishing. Jay and I continue to be friends.

Any time I get together with my High Park friends, we always reminisce about the days of our youth. We laugh and good-naturedly exaggerate certain stories. At times our stories bring tears to our eyes, tears that show joy and how much we miss each other. I wouldn't change much in my childhood life if I had to do it all over again, and I continue to treasure my childhood stories and the lessons they've taught me. Someone once said, "Good friends are like stars: you don't always see them, but you know they are always there."

I recently traveled back to High Park to visit the homestead and the community. I noticed that most of the homes have been upgraded, making the neighborhood, including our old house, much more attractive. Today the community has a sewage system and paved roads. But what was missing as I drove slowly through the neighborhood was the schoolhouse, the playground, our "field of dreams," and the noise of kids playing outside. The High Park School has been torn down and replaced by the High Park Fire Department Garage. The baseball and football fields have been replaced by homes. But I must admit the community looks basically the same as it did back in the fifties. Even though most parents are deceased, as I drove through the old neighborhood I thought for a moment I heard their voices and saw their faces along with the rest of my past, which remains imbedded in my heart and soul.

I know I can't go back, but as I sat in my parked car alongside the road of our old homestead I began to get sentimental recalling the journey of my childhood and the lessons learned. There I was, sitting and reminiscing about my youth. I thought to myself how quickly time had passed. At that special moment, I felt that I could walk down to my parents' house and visit my mom and dad. But then a slight breeze blew into my car window. It gently touched my face and brought me back to reality. That moment is now another—the latest—cherished High Park memory.

I started up the engine of my car and began driving slowly up Pine Street, remembering the neighbors by name, passing the former baseball field and school house, then circling around the entire neighborhood, and finally waving good-bye.

Lesson #50: There are so many life lessons to learn. Every day is an adventure that can and should bring happiness to a person's life.

A Closing Thought

I **wonder today if there** are any "High Parks" remaining in this great country of ours? I hope so because it would be sad for our youth today not to experience the friendships and wisdom gained from the events of a childhood like the one I experienced.

Recently I started my "bucket list" of things to do—things I have yet to do in my life, and I'm working on it. For example, I would like to travel to Italy to visit my grandfather's ancestors.

I believe in the wisdom of the saying, "Life is an adventure; don't procrastinate." Challenges create opportunities. That truth, among many others, is good to know as we make the most of life's SWEET FREEDOMS.

IF YOU'RE A FAN OF THIS BOOK, PLEASE TELL OTHERS...

✧ Write about *Sweet Freedoms* on your blog, Twitter, MySpace, or Facebook page.

✧ Suggest *Sweet Freedoms* to friends.

✧ When you're in a bookstore, ask them if they carry the book. The book is available through all major distributors, so any bookstore that does not have *Sweet Freedoms* in stock can easily order it.

✧ Write a positive review of *Sweet Freedoms* on www.amazon.com.

✧ Send my publisher, HigherLife Publishing, suggestions on Web sites, conferences, and events you know of where this book could be offered at info@ahigherlife.com.

✧ Purchase additional copies to give away as gifts.

CONNECT WITH ME...

To learn more about *Sweet Freedoms,* please contact me directly at:

Email: kengaudi@verizon.net
Web site: www.kengaudi.com

Sweet Freedoms Web site

Please visit **www.kengaudi.com** to learn more about *Sweet Freedoms* and Ken Gaudi. You may also order additional copies of *Sweet Freedoms* on the Web site for family and friends.